ON THE BALL?

How football can help your mental health

Paul Gaffney

ORIGINAL WRITING

ISBNs
Parent : 978-1-78237-548-7
epub: 978-1-78237-549-4
mobi: 978-1-78237-550-0
PDF: 978-1-78237-551-7

A cip catalogue for this book is available from the National Library.

Published by Original Writing Ltd., Dublin, 2014.
Printed by Clondalkin Group, Glasnevin, Dublin 11

With gratitude for life, love, family, friendship, psychology & sport.

For Geraldine and Amy.

Praise for *On the Ball?*

"Sport and especially one's local football culture is a microcosm of life as well as being something to which billions can relate. Paul Gaffney has built on the rich culture and scaffolding of football to illustrate many life lessons and identify solutions to the ebbs and flows of human happiness and suffering. This approach to mental health and well being will be immediately understood by the hundreds of millions of followers of the "world game" or "soccer", and also by followers of other sporting codes. Paul has selected football because it means so much to him and he has a deep understanding of it. The advent of this book fills a substantial gap in that many men, especially young men, for the first time perhaps can be helped to reflect on mental health challenges and the crises that life throws up in a way they can readily grasp without any resistance. However increasing numbers of women too will relate to the context and the content, while other men and women may prefer another approach. I have always seen parallels between the management of and participation in sporting teams and the workplace, and while some may still see this as simplistic, it contains a huge amount of truth and practical guidance. There are many special and varied features of the book and it is a pathway to a wider array of online and published resources. Another Irish gift to civilisation!"

Professor Pat McGorry, Department of Psychiatry, University of Melbourne & Executive Director, Orygen Youth Health

"This is a marvellous book, and all the better for being so short. By using his football metaphor Dr Gaffney has the knack of turning on the lights inside our heads, and making us want to use what we are reading about. By using the football metaphor Dr Gaffney appears to be targeting primarily young people, and perhaps young men, but I think it would be a pity if readers were confined to this group. This is a splendid book and the structure, which invites you to think more about what he says and follow up the leads he provides if you want to, works excellently".

Dr. William Davies, Academic Director, Association for Psychological Therapies (APT) & author of *Overcoming Anger & Irritability*.

"In *On the Ball?* We have a self-help book with a difference. Uncommon wisdom is conveyed to the reader in common language and through the medium of familiar football anecdotes. However, in marrying his passion for sport with his experience as researcher and clinician, Dr Gaffney does not skirt around or dumb down serious, sometimes painful topics. He does, however approach them with a light touch and sustained optimism. Each chapter is short enough to read on the bus home from work or before falling asleep after a busy day and ends, helpfully, with a brief list of things to try. When invited to provide this review, I assumed I was going discover a guys' book. Dr Gaffney reminds us, however, that women are fast becoming sports most ardent fans. They will find much that is relevant and useful in achieving personal fulfilment and healthy relationships. Meanwhile, for those of us who just like to talk about football, irrespective of what shape our lives are in, we can pretend we just picked up some reading from the sports shelves!"

Dr. Vincent Russell, Consultant Psychiatrist, Clinical Director (MHA), Cavan Monaghan Mental Health Service

"This book does a fantastic job of using examples from the game of football to illustrate how we can maintain and improve our day to day well-being. It is an honest, insightful book of wisdom and great practical value that everyone (including other professionals) can benefit from. This is a book that I will return to again and again for its practical exercises, countless inspiring quotes and eclectic recommended reading list."

Dr. Siobhain McArdle,
School of Health & Human Performance,
Dublin City University

"One of the most enduring things in football is the willingness of all involved to accept failure and disappointment and move on. There is a belief that even the worst situations can be remedied. Somehow things will get better next week, next month…next year maybe. In that sense football people are optimists. Paul Gaffney is one such person - and an experienced Clinical Psychologist as well. Writing in the language of the game, he draws a series of comparisons between football and life and shows how we can successfully apply the strategies of football to many of life's problems as well. The result? A short book filled with football, wisdom and hope."

Dr. Paddy Rudden, General Practitioner & Team Doctor

FOREWORD

On the ball? is a wonderful book that harnesses the power of football and all that is good about the game to deliver really useful life messages. In it, Paul Gaffney uses football analogies in a relevant and simple way to help people look after their mental health. The concepts of team, support, inspiration, playing with your head up, patience, persistence and bouncing back are just some of positive aspects of the game that he uses to get his point across so effectively.

For some years the FAI has been using football as a tool in communities to connect with people who would otherwise have little impulse to engage. The parallels with this book really struck me thinking about a project we started last year with our development officers and occupational therapists who work together through football to address mental health issues. The programme focussed on a sense of team, reaching out and getting fit and produced tremendous results. The key to its success was using the broad appeal of football to engage those involved in a way that would have been unlikely to succeed by other means. This book does the same and I have no doubt that it will become a valuable life changing resource for so many people.

John Delaney
Chief Executive
Football Association of Ireland

I have known Paul for over 10 years, during which he has delivered many informative and inspirational lectures to students on the Doctoral Course in Clinical Psychology. He is dual qualified as a Clinical and Counselling Psychologist and has gained a wealth of clinical experience in child and adolescent mental health settings. Like many clinical and counselling psychologists, Paul is an experienced and effective psychotherapist. However, what sets him apart from others is his ability to communicate with young people in a non-patronising manner. Through a number of interventions, he has helped develop in the recent past, he has conveyed complex psychological concepts to young people in a manner that is relevant and beneficial to them. Examples of such projects are the "Mind Yourself" mental health awareness initiative and the "Back of the Net" project run in conjunction with Dublin City University.

This most recent publication is in some ways a culmination of his recent efforts. "On The Ball?" is a user friendly book based on evidence based mental health enhancement strategies. The book uses the metaphor of football and youth friendly language. The text is easy to follow and every chapter contains "bite sized" ideas that can be readily put into practice. The book will be of interest to anyone working with young people and will help to engage young men in particular in thinking about their wellbeing and how to enhance it.

Dr. Kevin Tierney,
Trinity College, Dublin University.

Introduction

This is a book for anyone who is interested in football and in keeping well. As a psychologist lucky enough to work with people from many walks of life for almost 20 years, I have often thought about what had seemed most helpful for people and what had worked for individuals in specific circumstances. The curious thing about this is that during my training, when we were shown videos of famous and well known psychologists working with people, it sometimes actually appeared like they were just talking and listening to the other person (of course with some training I could later see the structure and process within this, and also realise that making it look easy was actually very hard work!).

Over the years, I realised that talking and listening is at the core of helping people and much of this is actually talking about every day events and the nitty gritty of each person's life. Some people I have worked with over the years have found it hard to talk about very painful or difficult issues and often begin each discussion by speaking about familiar topics or things that interest them. People seem to benefit most from working with a psychologist or therapist with whom they can build a good relationship, based on respect and a genuine interest in what the other person thinks, feels and says. Oddly enough, people seem more open and relaxed when I am not trying too hard to be a psychologist, but when I balance being a psychologist with actually being myself, and sometimes sharing some of my own experiences with the other person.

One of the most vivid experiences of my growing up was watching the FA Cup final on television in May 1975, when West Ham defeated Fulham by two goals to nil. I can remember much about that day. Seeing an entire game live (which was unusual on television in those days), being struck by how grand Wembley Stadium looked, how many people were there, how West Ham took the lead and finally scored a second goal to claim the cup. From that day on, I was going to be a West Ham fan and they were my team. But as you may well be thinking, if it was another team playing or winning that day, I may have become a fan of another team, and my life as a football fan may have taken another turn completely.

As a football fan, there is always something to talk about during the season - the league table, the international matches, the latest refereeing controversies, and in the close season, we have the transfer market and changes of manager. As a universal concept, football fans are both male and female, of all ages and living in countries all over the world.

I have been lucky over the past few years to work with colleagues in assessing whether football can also be good for your mental health. Through the "Back of the Net" project, we tested out this idea and found that when combined with individual exercise and a series of interventions influenced by a form of talk therapy called Cognitive Behaviour Therapy, football could be good for you and in an experiment the rate of depressive symptoms among the young men who took part fell by up to 45% (McGale, McArdle & Gaffney, 2011).

I have found it helpful to try and avoid where possible, universal truths or advice which may be true in every instance. Some of the following chapters focus on looking after yourself or "keeping a clean sheet". So many good teams build their game around a solid defence and build from the back, and this is a good message for life. In other chapters, I look at how you can make the most of your potential and try to have as good a life as possible, similar to pushing forward and scoring in football.

A key idea in this book is to try what works for you, not necessarily what everyone else thinks will work for you. No two people are exactly alike. However, it often seems to be the case that when a successful coach has used some new approach in achieving victory, it is hailed as the masterstroke of a genius. When a losing coach may have the used the same or similar approach, it can often be dismissed as silly or stupid. As a football fan myself, you will probably find this book opinionated, biased and subjective and I now take this opportunity to plead guilty on all counts!

You may find some of the chapters more interesting and applicable to you than others, and I encourage you to pick out what is most appealing and (hopefully) helpful to you. However, if you have any concerns at all about your health and wellbeing, please do contact your doctor or a mental health professional as soon as you can.

Paul Gaffney
May 2014

Contents

FIRST HALF

Chapter 1

FOOTBALL...A MATTER OF LIFE & DEATH

Football is really a simple game, you try not to concede goals and then try to score a goal when the opportunity arises. Life is also quite simple....we are here for a period of time, have an opportunity to make a life for ourselves (and our loved ones) and will eventually die.

I have been struck in recent years how complex and complicated many of the books and ideas on life and how to live it have become. While life can be rich, mysterious and have several layers, often the choices each of us may face can be quite basic and limited (for example, "do I stay in this job or go?"). And in any case, we cannot always influence many of the issues that can upset or annoy us, such as the economy, the weather, our family or our children!

In this scenario, it is understandable that we can become down and even hopeless, which is dangerous because hopelessness is often cited as a key factor in suicide and often plays a part in decisions to give up when we think we cannot do the job, pay back the loan, run the 10K race, get a place in the team, stay clean or sober and face the challenge in front of us.

I recall a situation when I was 22 years old and very unhappy, and probably depressed. I was in a situation where I was angry, sad and lonely, influenced in part by the death of my parents a few years apart. One morning a thought struck me that as both my parents had died at age 57, I might only have 35 years to go until I reached that age, or that two-fifths of my life could have already passed. While it took some time, the thought that every day was precious along with the knowledge that I had already experienced some hardship, helped take some of the fear and anxiety away and allowed me to make the decisions which I needed to make and get on with my life (with the priceless help of some people I trusted, including a psychologist).

In these uncertain times, many of us also worry about the present and the future, especially being able to earn a living to support ourselves (and if applicable, support our family and loved ones) as well as keeping ourselves healthy and well. Unfortunately, having success in the game and playing football at an elite and professional level does not mean players do not struggle with their own mental health issues, and we have witnessed some high profile tragic deaths in recent years, including the German goalkeeper Robert Enke. One way or the other, mental health is now an issue for football and sport in general, and we need to be more pro-active about openly tackling these issues, especially in raising awareness that any of us can suffer with our mental health if we find ourselves in the wrong place, at the wrong time or without the right supports and resources.

However, on a more optimistic note, I have always admired the experimental work conducted by the brilliant social psychologist, Daniel Gilbert, who has shown that we are unique among creatures on earth in having an ability to imagine what the future might be like and how we might feel about it. Gilbert suggests that while we can look into the future, we may not be so good at accurately imagining how we might feel about things then. His experiment looking at the responses of a group of people in the aftermath of experiencing a huge lottery win compared with a group of people who experienced a serious road traffic accident, is both surprising and curious (he found much less difference between these groups than you might expect), and this can serve to remind us that we really may not know how we feel about a situation until it actually happens, so maybe we should worry less about it in the first place.

Key Thought:

"Football is a simple game made complicated by people who should know better."

Bill Shankly

Looking for Inspiration?

Football regularly provides moments of inspiration which remind us how precious life is and how taking the gift of life and living it to the full is especially uplifting. This was well illustrated with Eric Abidal lifting the Champions League Trophy at Wembley on 28th May 2011, having played the entire 90 minutes of Barcelona's 3-1 win over Manchester United. Two months earlier Abidal was diagnosed with a tumour in his liver. Carlos Puyol handed Abidal the Captain's Armband and he lifted the trophy, pure class from both!

Things to try...

*Make a note today of all the things you are grateful for in life.

*Notice how much time you give to thinking about things than have not happened yet or may not happen.

*Think about the days/weeks ahead and think of something you are really looking forward to and something you are not looking forward to, rate each of them on a scale from 0 (dreading it) to 10 (cannot wait) now. After both have taken place, rate the events again from 0 (hated it) to 10 (loved it)... How do the pre and post event ratings compare?

*Ask yourself "What is the most important thing I have achieved in life so far?" and then remind yourself of this at least once a week, if you cannot answer this for yourself, ask someone whose opinion you trust.

If you liked this you can also look up...
Abrahams, D. (2012) *Soccer tough: Simple football psychology techniques to improve your game.* Birmingham: Bennion Kearny.

Bjergegaard, M. & Milne, J. (2013) *Winning without losing.* London: Profile Books.

Gilbert, D. (2006) *Stumbling on Happiness.* New York: Random House.

Kopp, S. (1972) *If you meet the Buddha on the road, kill him! The pilgrimage of psychotherapy patients* Palo Alto: Science and Behaviour Books.

Reng, D. (2011) *A life too short: the tragedy of Robert Enke.* London: Yellow Jersey Press.

Chapter 2

PRE-SEASON

The pre-season phase of each year brings with it the twists and turns of player transfers and changes of management, along with the infamous pre-season training, where players undergo intense and gruelling physical preparation for the schedule of games ahead. In this pre-season preparation, players get rid of the excesses of their time off and work on getting into shape for the season ahead. For each of us there are opportunities to do something similar when we make New Year resolutions or make promises to ourselves (and others) to eat or drink less, and to exercise more.

Psychological research has shown that there is a clear link between regular exercise and better mental health. In the "Back of the Net" project, my colleagues Nadine McGale, Siobhain McArdle and I discovered that taking regular exercise can have a significant benefit in terms of experiencing less depressive thoughts. Also, playing football adds value to the exercise element by helping the people in the study see more support available to them in the community than they may have previously been aware of.

For many of us, we can feel like we are in the pre-season mode much of the time... Wanting to and maybe knowing we need to get into better shape, ease off or alter our food/alcohol intake and wishing we were fitter and better conditioned. For some of us, putting a target in place may help, such as planning to do a run/

cycle/swim for charity or taking part in a team event, such as a football tournament. But what can we do on a daily basis to help, especially if we cannot focus on an upcoming event to help us get started?

The key seems to be finding a way of being in good physical condition that does not take over our lives, and can easily be integrated into our schedules and routines. In psychology, it is usually accepted that good mental health is built on good physical health and this, when combined with positive practices and daily habits, is sometimes called biological regulation. This refers not just to taking exercise on a regular basis, but eating adequately, getting enough sleep, and having some balance in these activities. If we cannot give our body what it needs, then how can our body keep carrying us around and always do what we want, when we want it?

It is also the case, that the mind itself needs periods of exercise and rest just like the body. So if you are playing video games/online football games which stimulate the mind and can challenge your hand eye co-ordination, then it is good to let the mind relax also, through relaxation of your preference and importantly by getting enough sleep, which nourishes the mind and helps us stay more balanced. I have always been surprised by reports of how much footballers play video games and use social media/surf the internet, but also how much they sleep, whenever they get the chance.

In my own life and work, and especially as I get older, getting the chance to relax is crucial. Important also is being able to integrate this relaxation into a daily routine as much as possible, lessening the chances of becoming exhausted or running on empty.

Key Thought:

"Rome wasn't built in a day. But I wasn't on that particular job."

Brian Clough

Looking for Inspiration?

Juanma Millo, has been an unofficial mentor to Pep Guardiola for many years, and is credited with influencing much of the playing philosophy exhibited by Pep's teams, particularly at Barcelona. When asked about mentally preparing players for matches, Millo has an unorthodox but intriguing take on tactics and strategy, insisting "You orientate people rather than order them. You balance, you adapt, you listen. Human beings are open; there is no answer that definitively closes any debate". Therefore the key idea is to prepare players to think in advance about options on the pitch, to assist them in making the right choice at the right time, alongside the physical preparations. This is a super skill in life too as we can never predict what may happen on any given day as we have to play each game as it unfolds in front of us.

Things to try...

*If you currently take no exercise at all, just try to fit in a walk as often as you can to begin with.

*If you have any concerns at all about your health or plan to take more exercise, please consult with your doctor.

*Try to ensure that you get a balance in activity/rest, with regular and scheduled time to do nothing.

*As a rule if you are not enjoying the exercise routine you have, try something else. It should as much as possible be enjoyable (although sometimes this enjoyment may come after the activity!)

*Keep a sleep or rest log, how much are you getting? You may need more sleep and the best way to manage this is to try to get to bed earlier each night and get into a better sleep habit.

If you liked this you can also look up...

Bregman, P. (2011) *18 minutes: Find your focus, master distractions & get the right things done.* London: Orion Books.

Lois, G. (2012) *Damn good advice (for people with talent).* London: Phaidon Press.

Lowe, S. (2012) The brain in Spain, in *The Blizzard, 1, 55-65.*

Mc, Gale, N., McArdle, S. & Gaffney, P. (2011) Exploring the effectiveness of an integrated exercise/CBT intervention for young men's mental health. *British Journal of Health Psychology, 16, 3, 457-471.*

Chapter 3

BUILD A SQUAD

One of the things I have noticed in the last few years is how so many books and programmes encourage us to be the best person we can and continuously self-improve. However, even if we were all to do our best in everything we do, not everyone can be successful and by definition, you cannot have winners without losers. Equally, there are times and tasks in life when we simply cannot do things (all) by ourselves, for example, when only a good plumber or electrician can fix a problem in your home. Trying to do everything by yourself, be that over-working, not delegating or putting yourself under too much pressure, is a prescription for misery.

What seems much more important in having happiness in life is not our *personal* ability, but our *interpersonal* ability. Having people we are close to, share something in common with and are committed to, can help us feel we belong, are valued and matter. This could be our families, colleagues, friends, team-mates or fellow supporters. The recession and financial downturn of the past few years reminds us that bad luck may be around the corner for any of us, but we actually need each other much more than we probably thought we did. In a world of less money and less time, good turns for your neighbour and helping out a friend (for example, by doing a chore for them, babysitting or taking their children on an outing) have become more significant.

Football also repeatedly shows us that it is the best team, not the team with the best individuals, who usually win out in the end. And in the modern era, of league, cup and European games, it is the club with the best squad who tend to be most consistent and who challenge most for titles.

Many of the people who I see as a psychologist, come for help in relation to difficulties with another person, including someone they are having conflict with, worries about a loved one or being bullied in a relationship, at school or in work. It always amazes me how unhappy some people can cause other people to be, and helping individuals in this situation usually involves encouraging them to understand, acknowledge and accept how and why their experiences upset them so much, and then teach them more effective skills and strategies to the better deal with situations. Happier people, like successful managers, have a good squad of people around them and use the bench when they need to.

One thing that can really help is an ability to imagine how it might feel if we were in the other person's situation, or "walking in their shoes", sometimes called emotional intelligence. This notion of emotional intelligence can be just as important as any other skill in life, and in business, can give people an especially strong advantage. This is a quality many great players share, as working closely as a team involves strong emotional understanding of each other in terms of not just where you will be positioned on the pitch or how you like to receive a pass, but how to get the best out of each other (just watch Xavi, Inesta & Messi of Barcelona interplay, sometimes without seeming to have to look up!)

One of the key ways to use your bench is to find and/or spend time with a mentor, or someone you look up to and who can guide you. When your chance comes, maybe you can be a mentor for someone else (so many successful managers speak about how winning as a mentor to a young team is more satisfying then being successful as players themselves). Remember; when you have a crisis, you may well have to empty your bench to get through it.

Key Thought

"A star can win any game; a team can win every game."

Anonymous

Looking for Inspiration?

Alex Ferguson's building and re-building successive teams at Manchester United from 1986-2013 has made him the most successful British manager in the modern era. Alongside Ferguson's tactical, talent-spotting and managerial ability, he was able to keep an absolute focus on the team as the most important thing, showing no difficulty in moving on a high profile player if he considered that this would improve the overall strength and cohesion of his squad. With this foundation, he was then able to focus on getting the best of the emerging youth talent, managing relationships with key players and making sure the club and team always came before any one individual during his 26 season reign.

Things to try...

Think about

*Who is on your bench among your family, friends and team mates?

*Who would you or have you turned to in a crisis?

*Consider who your mentor is, and seek their guidance regularly or seek a mentor out if you do not have anyone now.

*Who could you mentor or offer advice or guidance to? Could your experience and skill be helpful to someone else, possibly a younger person?

If you liked this you can also look up...

Brooks, D. (2011) *The social animal: A story of how success happens.* New York: Random House.

Ferguson, A. (2013) *My Autobiography.* London: Hodder & Stroughton.

Nugent, R. & Brown, S. (2008) *Football: Raise your mental game.* London: A. & C. Black.

Pearsall, P. (2005) *The last self-help book you'll ever need.* New York: Basic Books.

Chapter 4

STARTING 11

How often do you hear a football manager criticised for not being able to establish who the strongest starting 11 players in the team may be? This is a tricky question as a manager must take into account several factors including the opposition to be faced in the next game, the importance of the game, the performance of the players in recent games and training, and motivational and compatibility issues within the group of players. The key is finding the strongest and most suitable 11 players to take on the next challenge.

Within much of my training in clinical psychology, we were asked to look at situations and try to figure what was missing and/or what was wrong and what to do about it. Only in more recent years have we had more focus in psychology about looking for the strengths in a person/family/situation and encourage and build on these strengths, by pointing out what works well in some situations that could be applied to others and spotting skills that could be further developed with practice and encouragement.

Everyday life is often like this in that we face various challenges and difficulties, and in dealing with these it is important to be aware of our strengths, as well as what we are not so good at, for example confronting someone who has upset us or dealing with conflict among a group or team of people to which we belong. This also means being able to change tactics in the middle of a situation and remaining flexible and open to solutions, from wherever they may come. What I have found seems to work for many people is a high degree of emotional flexibility, so that adjustments can be made to help deal with the particular demands of a situation.

For example, in any given day we might do some or all of the following: Comfort our child who does not want to go to school, check out the water pressure for our parent or an older neighbour, have a meeting with our boss to address a tricky work issue, encourage a younger work colleague who is struggling with their new job, give a team-mate some financial advice on the phone, speak with our sister about her son's career, chat with a friend about the latest league games and talk to our partner about what needs done in the home. Each of these encounters requires a slightly different approach and our language, tone and emphasis will vary. Where we sometimes get into trouble is when we mistake the requirement for each situation... for example speaking to our boss in the same way we speak to our child! Emotional flexibility also tends to mean that we see the need to expect less of others (as they need to be flexible too) and coming to terms with the one constant in life - nothing stays the same for too long, and change is always happening.

However, if we are only flexible, we might not get the things that we need from each day, achieve our goals or get what we want. Have you ever got up in the morning with a mental list of things you need to get done, and realise in the evening that the day has got away from you and those things are still undone? What can really help here is to have a list of five or so daily habits that we will always try to do as a way of building a set of "good habits".

An example might be

1. Get some exercise, even just a walk.
2. Eat as much fruit and vegetables as you can.
3. Get some time to do something you really like (e.g. listen to music).
4. Do something good for someone else.
5. Do one task you normally want to avoid (e.g. opening bills/ clean car).

This can help us get more of what we need or want, as well as being a good foundation to add another shorter term target (such as doing more training or starting a new interest/hobby).

Key Thought

> *"There are positive and negative thoughts. And hey, it doesn't cost you a cent more to think positively."*
>
> Angelo Dundee

Looking for Inspiration?

After a distinguished playing career, David Moyes became manager of Everton in 2002 and left for Manchester United in the summer of 2013. At Everton, Moyes was consistently adept at making the most of his playing resources and playing to his team's strengths, despite operating with a smaller budget when compared with clubs with more financial clout. This is reflected in three League Managers' Association Manager of the Year Awards (2003, 2005, 2009) and 10 Premier League Manager of the Month Awards (the first in November 2002 and the most recent in March 2013). Despite difficulties at Manchester United, he remains one of the most highly regarded British managers.

Things to try...

*See if can you list 100 things you are good at or strengths you have? If you can list 100, could you add a few more? If you are struggling, ask someone you trust for a few suggestions for your list.

*Visit the Authentic Happiness website (details below) and complete questionnaires to look at your strengths and virtues, as well as lots of other positive psychology resources.

*See if you can come up with your own list of five daily habits, write them on a card to remind yourself each day and notice what happens.

If you liked this you can also look up...

Csikszentimhalyi, M. (2002) *Flow: The psychology of happiness: The classic work on how to achieve happiness.* London: Rider.

Leimon, A. & McMahon, G. (2009) *Positive psychology for dummies.* Chichester, West Sussex: Wiley.

Shenk, D. (2010) *The genius in all of us.* London: Icon Books.

www.authentichappiness.sas.upenn.edu

Chapter 5

WHAT ABOUT A CUP RUN?

One of the great things about football is the potential for a good run in a cup competition even if your team is struggling in other competitions and generally not playing well. A cup run also gives an opportunity to get ready for a specific type of competition, which is generally time limited with clear targets and aims.

In life, even if things are not generally going well for us at any point in time, an opportunity to focus on one specific area or project can be helpful, in a similar way that a cup run can. The aim is to have a specific target to focus on and work toward. A man I have seen for psychotherapy had lost his job and became deeply and seriously depressed, especially as he initially felt helpless in the face of what was happening to him and his family. He initially found the days long, and full of dark worries about how he would ever repay debts and what he could do to ever get back into the work-force.

What really impressed me about this man was his commitment to keep a focus on smaller achievable projects, despite a general sense of pessimism and hopelessness. Starting with getting to a local gym a few mornings a week and planning each day clearly, he undertook household tasks when the family were out, including cooking and cleaning, which he had not really done before. He also set out a number of targets, starting by negotiating with each creditor and ending up eventually retraining for a completely different career. It was a long and often difficult journey for him, but in the end he got there as each small project added more value to the next and all the while his mood, outlook and general health slowly improved.

I really admired this man's persistence on projects he undertook and how he saw them as more than just targets to reach for, and by trying to achieve these, he was already feeling a little better. For him the value was not in giving up, as without his projects, he would not have recovered in the way he did. He won back much of his self-worth (including identifying some new skills) in the process of trying to live out his values, and the fact that he was successful in the end was a bonus to him, but his journey back was perhaps his greatest learning.

Much of the landscape in our lives has changed since the world economy has become much more uncertain a few years ago, with catastrophic consequences in many countries, and in particular families and individual's lives. What seems so hard to take in is the scale of the financial meltdown, and how so many financial, economic and property experts (and governments) got it so wrong. I, like my colleagues, have seen several people and families over the past number of years who have found their lives falling in around them. One of the (often unspoken) fears these people have is that even if they can rebuild their lives now, that it could all be taken away again.

In the face of this suffering and distress, and as a non-economist, I have found some useful ideas from outspoken writer, Nassim

Taleb. In his book *Antifragile*, Taleb outlines how some people do not put their trust in the system as such and spread their resources more broadly (using the analogy of a bar-bell with weights at either end), and avoid putting their "all their eggs in one basket", so that if one area is wiped out, another may not be. He also shows how a life can be built so that one is less vulnerable to negative influence from more global factors, usually out of your control, with a healthy dollop of trusting your own ability and being suspicious of the prevailing wisdom at any particular point in time.

Therefore, the idea of a cup run, a specific project to undertake even if all else is not going to plan can be helpful, and remember, to save the season, you do not have to win the cup outright!

Key Thought:

> *"Knowing that people overestimate the impact of almost every life event makes me a bit braver and a bit more relaxed because I know that whatever I'm worrying about now probably won't matter as much as I think it will."*

Daniel Gilbert

Looking for Inspiration?

Bob Stokoe took over Sunderland in November 1972, at a time when they were close to the bottom of the then Second Division. However, by May 1973 Sunderland had won the FA Cup for the first time in 36 years, the first time a Second Division team had won the cup in 42 years. Stokoe's team beat Arsenal, Manchester City and Leeds on the way to the cup, and he is perhaps best remembered for his run onto the pitch at the final whistle and embrace with his brilliant goalkeeper, Jim Montgomery.

If you liked this you can also look up...
Forsyth, J.P. & Eifert, G.H (2007) *The mindfulness & acceptance workbook for anxiety.* Oakland, CA: New Harbinger.

Gladwell, M. (2013) *David & goliath.* London: Allen Lane.

Hardy, L. (2009) *Stokoe, Sunderland and 73: The story of the greatest FA Cup final shock of all time.* Orion: London.

Taleb, N.N. (2012) *Antifragile: Things that gain from disorder.* Penguin: London.

Chapter 6

TACTICS

One of the most common debates among football fans is around the idea of tactics, how the team plays and sets itself up. Thankfully, with a few easily learned phrases, any of us can sound like experts. Modern football tactics, and particularly team formation, have changed over the years, with much more of a focus on individuals working within the team system, as compared to the earlier formation styles, which featured more traditional roles and specialist positions. But change is constant and the 2013/2014 season appears to have seen a decline in the fortunes of teams who set out to dominate possession and wear opponents down (for example, Barcelona), in favour of teams who instead prioritise moving the ball quickly when they gain possession (for example, Real Madrid).

A crucial turning point for football came in the mid 1980's following a series of tragic incidents where people lost their lives at football grounds. Football simply had to change to survive and that has largely happened, by making grounds more comfortable and spectator (and family) friendly, making stronger efforts to remove racism from the game, more intense marketing of the football product and generally trying to make the game more attractive.

To my mind, psychology has made a similar journey, changing along the way to stay more relevant while assimilating emerging research findings. 100 years ago, the fledgling science of psychology was largely influenced by the thinking of Sigmund Freud, and helping people was based around long-term insight focused therapy or psychoanalysis. Since the 1930's and 1940's we had the behavioural psychology revolution, which highlighted the importance of how behaviour was learned and how behaviour could be influenced. Significantly, in the 1970's, a new approach evolved, which focused on how we learn about the world around us, and how our thinking about ourselves and others can influence us significantly. Building on the previous behavioural work, this approach, Cognitive-Behaviour Therapy (CBT), has become one of the most popular and broadly used approaches to trying to help people with psychological distress.

Since then, there have been many exciting developments, with a continued focus on helping people solve problems, in the context of a trusting relationship between the psychologist/therapist and the person seeking help. Ultimately, the vast majority of people come to individuals like me to help them solve a problem, and as such psychology (along with other disciplines) has tried to respond with problem orientated but solution focused ways of trying to help.

Among my favourite approaches at the moment are Solution Focused Therapy (which aims to help people with what they can do now, as opposed to what they can't), Eye Movement Desensitisation Re-processing (which aims to help people to come to terms with trauma), and Dialectical Behaviour Therapy (which aims to balance accepting the person as they are with helping them learn the skills necessary to change and cope better) There are several more approaches I have not mentioned, but if you have an issue you need help with, psychology usually has a tactical approach to help you try to deal with and (hopefully) overcome the problem.

Key Thought:

"A manager is a guide. He takes a group of people and says, 'with you I can make us a success; I can show you the way'".

Arsene Wenger

Looking for Inspiration?

As an Irish man, it is hard to forget the Jack Charlton era, when Ireland competed at the Euro Championships in 1988 and then at both the 1990 and 1994 World Cup. Jack brought his own brand of direct, uncomplicated football, and despite critics pointing out that the players were much more able than the approach suggested, Ireland were very difficult to beat, and while they did not score lots of goals, the tactics were efficient and functional, bringing Ireland its most celebrated football period. As Jack said himself "We inflict our game on people, put 'em under pressure".

Things to try...

*Look up (in my opinion) probably the best self-help website available at the moment, www.getselfhelp.co.uk, for lots of resources and ideas about helping you and your wellbeing.

*Check out the websites of the psychological societies in Britain (www.bps.org.uk) and Ireland (www.psihq.ie) for more details of psychological services and psychologists.

*Look out for the *Overcoming* series of books, published by Robinson, providing broad range of books written by experienced clinicians on a number of issues.

If you liked this you can also look up...

Harris, R. (2008) The Happiness trap: How to stop struggling and start living. Boston: Trumpeter.

Dweck, C. (2006) *Mindset: how you can fulfil your potential.* New York: Random House.

Postma, A. (2013) *The power of acceptance.* London: Watkins Publishing.

Shapiro, F. (2012) *Getting past your past: Take control of your life with self-help techniques from EMDR therapy.* Emmaus, Pennsylvania: Rodale.

Swales, M.A. & Heard, H.L. (2009) *Dialectical behaviour therapy: Distinctive features.* Hove, Sussex: Routledge.

Chapter 7

BOUNCING BACK

A number of seasons ago, Ian Dowie famously coined the phrase "bouncabackability" in a television interview to describe the resilience he needed from his players. This is a great word to describe the fighting qualities required from all serious players and strong teams. Things do not always go your way in football, and even the very best teams will endure periods where they are not playing well, are struggling for form and cannot seem to work effectively or string a run of results together. Indeed, in the modern game, it is very unusual for any one team to completely dominate the other in single games or throughout the season.

And so it is in life itself - for any one of us there may be times when we seem continually "under the kosh" and feel unable to cope and survive. In such situations, our "bouncabackability" will be put to the test. In terms of understanding the nature of suffering, helpful ideas come from a number of diverse sources, including Buddhism and spiritual/religious thinkers. Such approaches highlight how suffering is ultimately inevitable, and how we can sometimes add to our difficulties by being unable to accept the suffering that comes our way, asking "Why me?" As strange as it may sound, accepting suffering as it is in the here and now is often the first step to being better able to deal with what is happening.

As happens in football when one team is completely overwhelmed all over the pitch by a much better team for a period of time, we can also especially suffer in our own lives. If we do not have the resources to deal with the particular crisis or crises at hand, for example being able to pay debts we owe, complete a task within a time frame, or keep going with something, all we will want to do is to stop.

What can you do in a situation like this? The first thing is to confide in someone you trust in or who may be able to help, and see what they make of the situation and consider any advice they may give. This could also include speaking to your doctor or mental health professional if necessary.

Secondly, we can try to find some meaning in the situation and think about our values or what ideas are most important to us and give us some direction. One particular approach called Acceptance and Commitment Therapy (ACT), aims to help people take actions that are based on their values, even if these cause you suffering now (for example, having a row with your child over their not coming back on time because you value your role as a parent in keeping them safe), but which over time help you live to your values (and in this example hopefully get your child to adulthood in one piece). As football fans, we know first hand about suffering for our values, as most of us only ever tend to support one club for life, and continue to support that team as we value this part of our lives, despite the suffering that poor performances, relegation or defeat by bitter rivals can bring. Each season, only a very small number of supporters can enjoy victory as reflected in trophies and titles, with most of us ultimately experiencing defeat (again!).

Thirdly, it is worth reflecting on what elite athletes require for mental toughness; Sports and Exercise Psychologist Michael Sheard highlights that athlete's being confident in themselves and their ability and coping with (and perhaps expecting) setbacks as being crucially important in this regard.

As a psychologist, one of the ideas I have found most consistently helpful for people who are under pressure, is that of gradually changing habits, so that new more positive behaviours slowly but surely become part of everyday life. Blogger and author Leo Babuta on his blog *Zen Habits* and in his book, *The Power of Less*, suggests that we change just one habit at a time, and focus on this until we have it completely mastered (for example, getting up earlier in the morning, getting some exercise regularly, paying off debt) and before we turn to something else. In this way, in the eye of the storm, we avoid trying to change too many things at once and possibly failing at them all, making the situation even worse.

Key Thought

> *"Within your suffering you find your values, and within your values you find your suffering."*
>
> Steven Hayes

Looking for Inspiration?

Dave Jones, following a successful career as a professional footballer, managed football teams since 1995, both in and out of the Premier League, and in that time he has had several ups and downs. These range from bringing Stockport County to a League Cup Semi-Final and promotion in 1997, guiding both Wolves to the Premier

League in 2003 and Sheffield Wednesday to the Championship in 2013, winning the League Managers' Association Manager of the Year award in 1998, to being cleared during a trial on abuse charges in 2000. He suffered significantly on a personal level at this time by being suspended by Southampton in order to deal with the legal proceedings, followed by the death of his father shortly after details of the allegations became public. Jones continued to manage until late 2013, and what most impresses me most is his resilience and fighting spirit, over a prolonged period of time.

Things to try...

*Think about what you value or what is important in your life. Try to note down what you value most (or what matters most) at home, with friends or at work if you are in work?

*How have you bounced back before, what strategies worked then and could these work again if need be?

*If you are trying to make changes to your life it helps not to rush too much - try to do it one habit at a time and make sure you have got one habit established (for example stopping smoking or getting regular exercise) before you move on to the next habit.

*There is some strong evidence that experiencing suffering, hardship and adversity can actually help us as people and make us stronger, and this is really well explored by the books on post-traumatic growth by Stephen Joseph and hardiness by Paul Pearsall listed below.

If you liked this you can also look up...

Babuta, L. (2009). *The power of less: The 6 essential productivity principles that will change your life.* London: Hay House.

Hayes, S. (2005) *Get out of your mind and into your life: The new acceptance and commitment therapy.* Oakland, CA: New Harbinger.

Jones, D (2009). *No smoke, no fire: The autobiography of Dave Jones.* Birmingham: Know the Score Books.

Joseph, S. (2011) *What doesn't kill us: The new psychology of posttraumatic growth.* New York: Basic Books.

Pearsall, P. (2003) *The Beethoven factor: The new positive psychology of hardiness, happiness, healing and hope.* Charlottesville, VA: Hampton Roads.

Sheard, M. (2010) *Mental toughness: The mindset behind sporting achievement.* Hove, Sussex: Routledge.

Chapter 8

KEEPING A CLEAN SHEET

In football, not conceding goals or "keeping a clean sheet" is an absolutely essential ingredient, and is the basis of success for every winning team. Not conceding goals is not just the responsibility of the goalkeeper but of every player on the pitch, as every missed tackle or run by an opponent not tracked can lead to a scoring opportunity. Unless you are a team like Brazil, of whom it is traditionally said that if you score four, they will score five, not conceding goals, especially "soft" goals, is crucial.

In everyday life, trying to keep to the same principles is important as we do not want a situation where we are striving to do our best, make the most of our situation and look after those we care about, only to be undone by an error on our part, especially if we make the same mistake repeatedly. Of course things we'd rather didn't happen can always occur, but as in the unforced error in the game, if we have contributed to the situation it always seems worse.

In my work I have come across situations where people have put themselves in compromising situations through taking unnecessary risks or chances. This can range from not taking care of their health right through to much more dangerous risks, such as driving under the influence of alcohol or drugs, being violent towards others, or getting involved in crime. Many of these behaviours may be accompanied by an underlying addiction issue or by chronic impulsivity. In this regard, the internet is a mixed blessing for people with addictive tendencies toward on-line gambling and pornography in particular.

These problems need to be addressed to get to the core of the issue. Perhaps it is coincidence, but I have noticed that many former professional footballers, especially younger players, appear to come to the attention of the media in relation to developing addiction problems or even becoming involved in crime. Perhaps it is difficult to leave an exciting and adrenaline fuelled career behind, and return and/or get used to a more humdrum existence for these individuals, in whom the media tends to keep an interest in long after their playing days. However, football also features a number of people who have addressed and overcome their own demons, especially in the area of addiction and compulsive behaviours.

Football, and sport in general, reminds us that despite their efforts, individuals and teams rarely get what they might deserve in terms of success and most football fans tend to repeatedly talk about the trophies their teams lost as much (or more) as they ones they won, for example Liverpool coming up just short in the 2014 Premier League title race. However, we all sometimes fail to come up to our own standards and fall down, but getting up again (and again and again) and trying to take some learning from our failure (if there is any), is the key.

Another difficulty any of us can experience is overly negative or toxic people who can drain us of energy and focus on the negative side of life (or indeed, our negative side). Avoiding such people if you can helps, and if you cannot avoid them try to limit your time with them and try to plan how you can keep yourself out of harm's way in their company, including not getting into conversations that you do not want to.

Key Thought

"The goalkeeper is the jewel in the crown and getting at him should be almost impossible. It's the biggest sin in football to make him do any work."

George Graham

Looking for Inspiration?

Oisín McConville, while being a noted footballer, made his name as one of the finest Gaelic Footballers Ireland has produced, building a reputation throughout a lengthy career as a classy forward with an eye for goal. McConville showed remarkable character to score the winning goal for Armagh in the 2002 All-Ireland Gaelic Football Final, having earlier missed a penalty, to help them win their first national senior title. More recently, he revealed that he has been struggling throughout most of his career with a long term gambling addiction problem which had led to debts of a six figure sum. Following treatment for his addiction, McConville has now become an addiction counsellor and gives regular talks on the subject, shining a light on a problem that is often hidden or not discussed, including among sports people.

Things to try...

*Have a look at Gaelic Football and Hurling if you get a chance, both games have no offside, physical contact is allowed and players are amateurs - no such thing as scoreless draws and you cannot take your eyes off the game! Ideally look up the 2013 All Ireland Senior Hurling Final Replay between Cork and Clare on You Tube, reckoned by many to be the finest final ever!

*Is there one thing you can do today to help you "keep a clean sheet", by removing a habit or part of your life that can cause problems for you?

*Is there anything you do in life that you would not feel comfortable telling your children or loved ones about? If so, maybe you could try to get this out of your life.

*Difficulties with addiction are very difficult to overcome and people who overcome addiction issues in my experience almost always need both professional help initially to change their behaviour and ongoing support or fellowship by being part of a group to adapt to a new lifestyle without the addiction issue. If you are struggling with an addiction issue, start by talking to someone you trust and/or a professional such as your General Practitioner.

If you liked this you can also look up...
Davies, W. (2000) *Overcoming anger and irritability: A self-help guide using cognitive behavioural techniques.* London: Robinson.

Merson, P. & Allen, M. (2012) *How not to be a professional footballer.* London: Harper Sport.

McConville, O. & McKenna, E. (2007). *The Gambler: Oisín McConville's story.* Edinburgh: Mainstream Publishing.

Sutton, R. (2007). *The no asshole rule: Building a civilised workplace and surviving one that isn't.* New York: Business Plus.

Chapter 9

They've all gone quiet

"They've all gone quiet over there" can sometimes be the chant directed from a group of fans whose team has taken the lead toward the fans of the opposing team. Indeed, many coaches talk about the need to score early to help "silence the crowd" when they visit particularly daunting away grounds.

However, more recent developments within psychology suggest that "quietness" and mindfulness meditation have very positive benefits for your success and even happiness in life. Mindfulness aims to help us more fully pay attention to the present moment, without being overwhelmed by events of the past or overanxious about the future.

One of the qualities that distinguish great players from good players is the ability to both appear to have plenty of time on the ball and yet rapidly and effortlessly make the right decision in terms of picking out a pass, dribbling and/or having a shot. Basically, this could be described as playing in the moment. The idea of being able to play in the moment is in many ways similar to the idea of being mindful, and mindfulness has become very popular in recent years within psychology and mental health.

Based on the Buddhist philosophy of being aware of each moment - as opposed to the opposite which is not to be aware and could be called mindlessness - this is not only an important skill but also a way of looking at the world. In many ways the mind is an extra sense along with smell, hearing, sight, taste and feel and this idea of having presence of mind simply means living in the moment without worrying too much about what has happened before (e.g. mistakes we may have made earlier in the game or in our lives) or fears of what may come next (e.g. concerns about how the opposition will play in the second half or what might happen in our own lives).

One of the most important elements here is to be comfortable on the ball and to be comfortable within ourselves. Jon Kabat Zinn talks about the most important attitudes when being mindful through his highly successful Mindfulness Based Stress Reduction (MBSR) programmes. These include being non-judgemental by seeing a situation as it is without rushing to compare or evaluate it. When we are distressed, many of our thoughts are often evaluations and judgements, including comparing ourselves to other people, with how we used to be or with how we would like to be.

Patience is a key element in terms of mindfulness, not rushing things along before we are ready and accepting how we are in that moment. Thirdly, the idea of beginners mind, where life is full of possibilities whereas with an expert mind, there tend to be fewer possibilities. Trust is important in terms of not just trusting those around us, but also trusting our own instincts. Non striving focuses on how we are already in the here and now without wishing we were perfect or different, and is important in terms of being able to start out accurately from the place we are at now.

Acceptance relates to taking things the way they are now, and being content with things without wishing that they were better. How often have you seen a TV interview where a manager is complaining that the team would perform better had more funds been available to strengthen the squad or if key players had fewer injuries? Acceptance begins with where we are at this moment in time. I often think of Liverpool's second half performance in the 2005 Champions League Final as an example of how important the accepting of the situation is in the first place, whereby allowing the team to play in a more focused way helped them to overcome exceptional odds in the second half, extra time and penalties.

Finally, non-attachment relates to the Buddhist idea that nothing is permanent and that things change. There are many things in life which we cannot hold on to, including people we love or our speed as younger players. However, as we grow older we can use our skills in a different way in order to maximise our strengths.

Key Thought

"We love football that is attractive, attacking and easy on the eye. When you win playing like this it's twice as satisfying."

Xavi Hernandez

Looking for Inspiration?

Few players better reflect the idea of being able to play in the moment than Xavi Hernandez from Barcelona. It helps, of course, that Xavi has superb technical ability and plays as part of the supremely talented and attack-minded Spanish and Barcelona teams, yet every time I watch him he seems so completely at ease with himself, focusing only on the task in hand and having enough time on the ball to almost always select the correct option. While not the youngest, tallest or fastest player, Xavi has consistently being a play-maker of the highest quality, has won more trophies than any other Spanish player in history and was voted onto the FIFA World Team for six consecutive years (from 2008 – 2013).

Things to try...

*Try to be more aware of what is happening around you through mindfulness, and one of the best recent books in this area is *Mindfulness for Health*, in the list below, which comes with a useful CD to help you practice. Alternatively, any book or online talk by Jon Kabat Zinn, who is credited with introducing mindfulness to the West, is also a really good resource. Have a look at the mindful living website below for more details.

*The idea of mindfulness is an ancient one. A courageous Vietnamese monk, Thich Nhat Hanh, writes really well about mindfulness and how it can help in all sorts of situations. His many works are well worth a look, particularly the book mentioned below.

* Simply taking time each day to do nothing and just focus on your breathing for a minute can help you to calm, focus and take a mental break from what is going on around you. Try to focus on doing things in a more mindful way...eat your meals without the television on or drive without music on in the car...

you will be surprised at what you may notice and how you may actually feel calmer.

*Next time you watch Spain or Barcelona play; keep an eye on Xavi's movement and his vision both on and off the ball - amazing!

If you liked this you can also look up...

Burch, V. & Penman, D. (2013). *Mindfulness for health: A practical guide to relieving pain, reducing stress and restoring wellbeing.* London: Piatkus.

Cain, S. (2012). *Quiet: The power of introverts in a world that can't stop talking.* London: Penguin.

Nhat Hanh, T. (2008). *The miracle of mindfulness.* London: Rider.

Kabat-Zinn, J. (2013). *Full catastrophe living (updated & revised).* New York: Bantam Books.

www.mindfullivingprograms.com

Chapter 10

PLAY WITH YOUR HEAD UP

One of the key elements in any relationship, be it in our personal lives or with our colleagues on a team, is communication. This includes being able to clearly communicate with each other, especially when we are under pressure in a difficult situation, but also involves a willingness to look to communicate, understand and see what our colleague is signalling to us and to listen to what is being said. Equally, how often have you seen a team concede a goal because an incoming ball was diverted into the net as the goalkeeper's shout went unheard? Or when a dangerous back-pass was played because the defender was not looking up and around for dangers? Or even how a player stretches to barely touch a near post cross when a colleague in a great far post position is screaming for the ball to be left to them?.

Players on successful teams focus endlessly on communication, including sometimes having a specific communication code which cannot be interpreted by others and also focusing on key areas such as allowing team players to speak and to clear the air, expect and plan for differences of opinion within the dressing room and negotiate difficulties, especially when the team is under pressure or having a poor run of form.

I came across a good example of this many years ago when a team had a rule that at half time in each game they would encourage players to have a discussion for 5-7 minutes amongst themselves before the Manager joined them, which then allowed him to reflect on what had been said, describe any changes required and give the team directions to go and play for the second half. The ability of players to listen and freely express themselves has always been appreciated as it not only allows players to feel heard and validated but also prompts interesting ideas around how the team could play better during this process. For me, it is no coincidence that the most successful and fulfilled people I have come across in life tend to be very good and natural communicators, learning to balance the need to speak effectively and decisively when required, with simply listening and reflecting back when that is necessary too (according to one such person, this highlights the fact that we have one mouth and two ears!)

For parents, the most important mentoring role is with your children and this can perhaps be the most rewarding, and at times most challenging role anyone can have in life. Parenting is a little like a football performance. When you are getting it right, it looks and feels easy and natural, but like a team in a poor run of form, when it is not going well it can be painful, frustrating and upsetting. In modern times, parenting has almost being raised to a profession, with so many opinions existing on what good parenting is and how it should be done.

However, every parent, child and parent-child interaction is different and what I notice works for some people may not work for others. But the essential elements appear to be related to good communication channels remaining open, especially during periods of turbulence or agitation in the relationship, and individuals not "burying their heads in the sand" but endeavouring to play with their heads up.

Key Thought

"Young players need freedom of expression to develop as creative players... they should be encouraged to try skills without fear of failure".

Arsene Wenger

Looking for Inspiration?

Lionel Messi is not only regarded as perhaps the best footballer in the world (at the very least in the top three), but also brings his own humility and willingness to be a team player to the table, making it a potent package. Messi received a diagnosis of a growth hormone deficiency at age 11, leading to Barcelona offering to pay for expensive treatment if Messi moved to Barcelona, which he then did with his father, who had been his first coach. Messi would probably not be the player he is today without the mentoring of his father from the beginning in Argentina and with the significant assistance of Barcelona since his move there. He stands out for me not just because of his incredible skill and courage, nor because of the unprecedented run of records broken and awards won, but for his team focus and his tracking back and working hard for his team, especially in how he provides opportunities for colleagues to score.

Things to try...

*Think about ways you can play with your head up? This could include listening to conversations you do not like but can at least hear what is being said and take part in this. Do you ever bury your head in the sand? Does this work for you?

* One of the biggest mistakes we make in relationships is reacting to a situation and then saying how this makes us feel, this can often cause damage. Next time you get really upset with someone try to do what you need to do to change the situation, but do not say how this makes you feel, only later when you are less upset and the situation is less heated, then say how you felt at the time. This tends to be easier as it may leads to a discussion and not prolong a confrontation which may get you nowhere anyway.

*As a parent, remember the crucial role you play (even if your children do not always appreciate this) as the first and most important mentor (as with Lionel Messi and his father).

*Can you think of the best advice you were ever given? Who gave you this advice? Could this help someone else now if you were to share it?

If you liked this you can also look up...

Abrahams, D. (2012). *Soccer tough: Simple football psychology techniques to improve your game.* Birmingham: Bennion Kearny.

Balauge, G. (2013). *Messi* London: Orion Books.

Davies, W. (2013) *The RAID course handbook.* Leicester: APT Press.

Chapter 11
BACK OF THE NET

While life will have both positive and enjoyable experiences along with negative and painful times for us all (hopefully less negative and more positive), it is important to recognise and acknowledge what we already have and appreciate the blessings, people and gifts in our lives. Of course, without something to compare the bad times with, there would not be good times as such.

Celebrating what we have and have been given is a quality the happiest people I know all seem to possess, even if I think about their lives in terms of what they have lost (for example, loved ones who have died) or what has been taken away (loss of some functioning with advancing years, or loss of a job and business), often in unfair or unjust circumstances. Martin Seligman, a positive psychologist who focuses on what we already have and can be grateful for, has shown that an attitude of gratitude towards life can enhance our mental health and generally tends to be much more useful than focussing on what's missing or what's wrong. For example, often in psychology the common language speaks of deficits or disorders (for example, Attention *Deficit/* Hyperactivity *Disorder* or Conduct *Disorder).*

Keeping a simple journal or noting down each day what has gone well and what you are grateful for, can always be useful and keeping it simple if you can (for example a word/view/song) to remind you of good times and good moments, can be helpful as well. Nurturing and being kind to yourself is also crucially important, as sometimes just getting up and facing each day can be an achievement in itself. It is natural and understandable that we all have bad days, good days and better days, and trying to learn from this is important - for example, asking ourselves in such times are we tired and do we need to take a little more time to ourselves? Or perhaps we need to look at an old problem in a new way? However, if strong feelings of sadness, fear, shame or worry do persist, then it is time to talk to someone you trust and if necessary, please seek professional help.

It is important to note here that when we talk of "professional help", many people can see this as some kind of admission that there must be something really wrong with them, their family and/or their children. Sometimes seeking help does end up in a specific diagnosis, which is really a psychological way of helping to tell your story and point out what help is needed and from whom. However, the opportunity to speak with a stranger is often what is found to be most helpful, especially as many people come in with a potential solution in mind. The professional often recognises such solutions as good options, and often the person may say *"that is exactly what my partner and/or family say as well"*!

During 2012, after some family bereavements and a general sense of being more tired than usual, I found myself going back to individual psychotherapy, which for many psychologists is an important part of their training. Simply going to speak to another psychologist and being allowed to have that time and space for yourself was very important to me in 2012 and I now do this on a monthly basis. It is useful on many levels, including experiencing what people who come to see me may feel when they meet someone like me. It also allows my psychologist to challenge me on things if needed and permits me to experience the full range of feelings which may not seem safe or fair to bring up or work through in other settings (for example, at work, with my family and friends).

This brings us to the idea of flow and being able to move and push things forward in a really positive way. The best example of this for me is Ian Holloway and his contribution to football over the years. Ian Holloway has experienced his fair share of ups and downs in his career as a manger, and yet seems to treat success and failure as both passing fads (which essentially they both are). In doing so, he goes out each day with a smile on his face and remembers that his behaviour and attitude (and famous sound-bites) will impact on all of those around him, whilst not forgetting the folksy wisdom of his parents and focusing on the needs of his family.

Key Thought

> *"There was a spell in the second half when I took my heart off my sleeve and put it in my mouth."*

Ian Holloway

Looking for Inspiration?

Ian Holloway has been a hero of mine for many years and has gained a reputation for playing positive football, often with meagre resources. Despite good success (most recently bringing

Blackpool and then Crystal Palace up from the Championship to the Premiership), he has also had his share of setbacks and disappointments, leaving Crystal Palace just a few months after bringing them up to the Premiership in the 2013/2014 season, and then bouncing back by keeping Millwall safe in the Championship. The one constant in his career however, has been his ability to get the best out of players (often when resources are stretched), a tendency not to take himself too seriously (and be hilarious in the process) and a capacity to relate to the fans who come to matches and pay the wages of all involved - a feature not always found in the modern game.

Things to try...

*For a recent "back of the net" moment I think about the wonder goal scored by Irish player Stephanie Roche for Peamount United - check it out for yourself on You Tube!

*I try once a week (usually on a Sunday evening) to make a note of one thing I am happy with/thankful for and then one thing I can learn from (usually a mistake or error of judgement made that week). I find it can help me both reflect on the week that has past and focus on the week to come; this may also be helpful for you too.

*Try to make a note of things you are grateful for and read over them regularly.

*Dr. Steven Peters has been associated with the unprecedented medal success of British athletes at the 2012 Olympics and especially with British professional cycling. Notably, he has worked with multi-world championship winning snooker player Ronnie O'Sullivan and with Liverpool FC, and he is now to work with the England football team. His fascinating book is well worth a read.

* Have a look at the Ian Holloway books listed below...

If you liked this you can also look up...

Dobelli, R. (2013) *The art of thinking clearly.* London: Sceptre.

Holloway, I. & Clayton, D. (2008) *The little book of Ollie'isms* Swindon: Green Umbrella Publishing.

Holloway, I., Clayton, D. & Francis, G. (2011) *Ollie: The autobiography of Ian Holloway (Updated Version).* Chelmsford: G2 Entertainment.

Peters, S. (2012) *The chimp paradox.* London: Vermilion.

Seligman, M (2002) *Authentic happiness: Using the new positive psychology to realise your potential for lasting fulfilment.* New York: Simon & Schuster.

SECOND
HALF

Chapter 12

IT'S A GAME OF TWO HALVES

Every game of football is different and the balance of play and scoring opportunities can fluctuate between the teams at various points in the match.

In many ways this is reflected in everyday life itself and the relationships that we are involved in. In every relationship, be it with our partner, family, work colleagues, friends and team mates, we feel very close to a person or group of people at times, and at other times we can feel distant from that same person or group of people. Our feelings can vary from love and being loved to hating and being hated, and probably everywhere else in-between. Everyday, persistent differences, niggles, annoying habits or grudges can cause difficulties as well as more major let-downs, disagreements, losses and betrayals.

Psychologist Paul Pearsall speaks about the importance of our relationship with others being just as significant as the relationship with ourselves, and unhappiness can often come about as a result of having problems in relation to, or with, other people, including family, friends, team mates and colleagues. However, it does seem natural and to be expected that since we all change somewhat ourselves over time, our relationships with other people will not remain exactly the same either.

Rarely do we continue to relate to, or get on with other people the way we always did. For example, when we are children we relate to our parents very differently as compared with how we would relate to them when we reach adulthood. Indeed, as parents become older, the "children" may assume more of a care-giving role, a swapping of the child/parent roles almost, and a full 180 degree turn is often seen across the lifespan.

In my everyday work with people, especially with younger people, it is important to reflect on the idea that sometimes the most effective relationships are ones where conflict is inevitable (but combat is optional!). For example, if a friend asks us not to let them drink too much alcohol on a night out and later on we attempt to do this, or if we try to point out to a loved one how they are being taken advantage of in a particular relationship, our interventions may not always be welcome, no matter how well intentioned we may be. To care about or to love someone means that we will feel strongly about that person and their wellbeing. We can understand the person, have a good enough idea how they feel and usually be on good terms with them, yet still have times when there is a misunderstanding or disagreement, and this may be unavoidable.

However, these situations offer great potential for us to learn something about ourselves and our relationships. Aside from encouraging the repair and (hopefully) the eventual restoration of relationships - which is a crucial skill for all of us - these relationships mirror what life is really like, where there is an understanding of what each us brings to a relationship, for example an employer pays an employee to do a job, but if either work or pay is withheld, then there are problems. Similarly, the ability to repair relationships within teams is also crucial, especially before people take sides and a clique culture becomes more pronounced.

In my work as a psychologist, I see better outcomes when a relationship goes through ups and downs, because this is what happens from time to time in most relationships. What we can learn for the future is how to stick to good habits in relationships. One important example of this is to always encourage communication, even if we know we may not like what is being said and/or to not completely judge ourselves or another person on the basis of one situation.

When I think about a game of two halves, one of the greatest comebacks was hatched at half time in the 2005 Champions League Final in Istanbul. After a torrid first 45 minutes Liverpool appeared out-thought, out-fought and were losing three goals to nil. It is hard to get a sense of what exactly went on, but keeping to a strong work-rate, some tactical and formation changes and an urgent need for an early goal, Liverpool emerged after extra time and penalties winning the Champions League.

Key Thought

"Character is like a tree and reputation is like its shadow. The shadow is what we think of it; the tree is the real thing."

Abraham Lincoln

Looking for Inspiration?

Stephen Gerrard's 'Man of the Match' role in the Champions League final of 2005 is still remarkable, even when looking back at the footage of that game a number of years later. I will never forget watching the first half of the game and thinking how gutted all those Liverpool fans who had made the trip to Istanbul must feel, with a real hammering looking likely at half-time. Yet, in an incredible second half, Liverpool scored three goals in six minutes and forced the game to extra-time before winning it out 3-2 on penalties. Gerrard was inspirational - scoring the first goal, earning the penalty leading to the third goal, and not least by providing leadership throughout.

Things to try...

*Consider some other dramatic football comebacks, for example the 1999 Champions League Semi-Final when Manchester United overcame Juventus, or the 2013 FA Cup tie where Arsenal won 7-5 to beat Reading who had lead by 4-0...do you have your own favourite? Or maybe you played in or watched a remarkable comeback?

*Repairing relationships is a crucial skill to develop. If you have hurt the feelings of someone you care about it is usually best to apologise as soon as you can (only of course if you actually are sorry!). Equally, if you feel someone has hurt you, tell them as soon as you can and give them a chance to deal with your issue. Try not to let things fester (e.g. telling someone else how much the person hurt you before you tell the person in question).

*To be effective in relationships, particularly in work or sport, *respect* in relationships tends to be more important than always *liking* a colleague or manager. There are always people who we will not get on with or who do not quite like us, but if we at least try our best in what we are aiming to achieve together, they can at least have reason to respect us and our efforts.

If you liked this you can also look up...

Beck, A.T. (1988) *Love is never enough: How couples can overcome misunderstandings, resolve conflicts, and solve relationships through cognitive therapy.* New York: HarperPerennial.

Gerrard, S. & Winter, H. (2006) *Gerrard: My autobiography.* Bantam Press; London.

Sutton, R. (2012) *Good boss, bad boss: How to be the best...and learn from the worst.* New York: Business Plus.

Chapter 13

How much do you want it?

It is traditional for many of us to state our good intentions at the beginning of each new year and make resolutions about becoming thinner, lighter, faster or richer (to name but a few). What tends to be the key difference between those of us (including myself) who annually make and break resolutions and those of who tend to succeed at them is the ability to persist in aiming for the goal or target when things become too painful, inconvenient or awkward.

In overcoming our resistance to make changes that we think might help us and improve our lives it is useful to focus on two key questions *What specifically will I do?* and *Why will this make a difference?*

"What specifically will I do?"

The clearer we are about what we need to do and when we need to do it, the more benefit we will gain and the more efficient we will be. For example, under the direction of Pep Guardiola, Barcelona had a reputation for being very difficult to beat due to their ability to retain possession for lengthy periods of time, to help create more scoring opportunities for themselves and to deny their opponents possession of the ball. A key element of this plan was the six seconds rule where Barcelona put massive focus into getting the ball back from their opponents within the first six seconds of losing possession. This can disconcert opponents and, if dispossession happened in a forward position, could actually create a goal scoring opportunity for Barcelona.

Secondly, have a realistic timeframe for making and sustaining changes. Does this sound familiar? I'll make a resolution to run 10km twice a week, plan this by buying new kit and trainers, run 3km the first day but retire as it begins to rain. I run 1km a week later but feel very tired and so give up. Thus my attempts end with me saying to myself "I'll never be able to run 10km". The major problem here is the way in which I planned the 10km. Following the principles of the "Ladder of Achievement" (Davies 2013), I would instead mark out the steps in reverse... Step 6-run 10km, step 5 – run 7km, step 4 – run 4km, step 3 – run 2km, step 2 – walk 2km and step 1- buy gear and plan route (and find someone to run with). Then I start at step one and work my way up the ladder. By using this strategy, even if I only get to step 3 on the ladder, I will have done something good for myself and my health.

Thirdly, as a match develops, one useful strategy for teams is to play the game in 10 minute segments, whereby each 10 minute period is treated as an entity in itself. As such, if we do well enough across the 10 minute segments we have a decent chance of winning the game. And if we have a difficult 10 minutes (for example, concede a goal, have a player sent off) we simply need to refocus to win the rest of the remaining minutes. In everyday life, this can mean getting through one day at a time, or in difficult times, getting through the next hour.

"Why will this make a difference?"

This is an equally critical question as at moments of doubt or uncertainty about making changes, the reasons behind our motivation become very important. This is basically asking for whom and why am I doing this? Staying motivated is difficult, but if we feel it will make a difference to the lives of our loved ones, then we can see a bigger picture. A friend of mine who gave up smoking said his main motivation at really difficult times of craving was thinking about his children having a father for longer, and him being more physically fit and having more energy to enjoy the time he had with his children. In my own life, I am aware that trying to look after my fitness will (hopefully) benefit my family in my being around for longer and being in better shape to enjoy life.

Our ability to change things is also helped by recognising the things we are currently doing that we would like to continue to do, so that existing good habits or helpful strategies are built upon. When we need to motivate other people, Dan Pink points out that, apart from fairly straight-forward manual tasks, people tend to be much more motivated in situations where they have some control over their environment, are able to develop skills and fulfil their potential. Thus, the older "carrot and stick" approaches have less relevance in the modern world. This is highlighted by practices in Google where employees are actually encouraged to spend some time working on their own ideas and projects, alongside the work they are required to do as per their job description. If we want to keep people more motivated in a team or group situation, give them some independence and individual responsibility, with an opportunity to bring their own individual strengths to bear on things.

Key Thought

"Start where you are. Use what you have. Do what you can."

Arthur Ashe

Looking for Inspiration?

Roy Keane had a colourful and controversial playing career beginning with his local team in Cork, later progressing on to Brian Clough's Nottingham Forest and ending up as the midfield general and leader in Alex Ferguson's Manchester United. Stories of Keane's virtual obsession with preparation for games and taking personal responsibility are almost legendary now, but both his driving force and meticulous mind for being ready for each game was a key component in United's success during that period, as well as being a factor in his managerial career since then.

Things to try...

*Be really specific about what you want to achieve and why?

*Try to learn to use the ladder of achievement as outlined above to tackle more challenging tasks or projects, and be patient with yourself in using it as small, slower changes generally tend to stand the test of time better

*For whom would you make changes in your own life, if not for yourself? Why would this be important? For whom would life be different if you could make the changes you wanted?

*Sometimes two heads can be better than one - if trying to change a habit, find a partner who would also try to change one at the same time and you can offer each other encouragement on the way.

* Look up the books below for advice and inspiration, especially the *Changing for Good* book.

If you liked this you can also look up...

Davies, W. (2013) *The RAID course handbook.* Leicester: APT Press.

Prochaska, J., Norcross, J. and DiClemente, C. (1994) *Changing for good.* New York, Avon.

Pink, D.H. (2010) *Drive: The surprising truth about what motivates us.* Edinburgh: Canongate.

Chapter 14

Practice, practice, practice

The weather... the pitch... the referee & officials... injuries to key players... the opposition... the scheduling of the game... the floodlights. These are just some of the excuses which can be trotted out when our team does not win or when the result has gone against us. The key to success in football (and in sport and life) is the ability to control what we can control, especially in how we prepare for events and to practice what we know will most likely happen. To not do this would be like going into a big game without rehearsing our set pieces, including corners kicks, free-kicks or penalties.

The basic difficulty in football, as in life, is that we actually have very little control over many of the factors that influence our fortunes. As a psychologist, the sadness, pain and trauma I see in peoples' lives can seem very overpowering and I sometimes feel helpless in the face of the adversity some people have endured (but more often than not, feel humbled by their resilience and courage in the face of this adversity). In this regard, practice helps us not just to prepare, but can focus our nervous energy and anxiety into something constructive by practising often and well.

The danger for us all is that, if we become overwhelmed by how little we can control, this could lead to a cycle of negativity, pessimism and most dangerously, hopelessness. On the other hand, we do not want to be encouraging people toward what is sometimes termed "blue sky thinking", where relentless (and perhaps, inaccurate) optimism is encouraged and people are told that things *have* to get better. This can be even more damaging than unrelenting pessimism.

What seems to be more helpful is to have a generally optimistic outlook, with an acknowledgement that we will not always get our way, and sometimes things can go wrong, very wrong. However, in very difficult situations, having the resources to cope is crucially important. I was involved in designing and setting up a community intervention called Mind Yourself (see website details below) which included more than 9,000 young people, where we looked at what optimism and pessimism were and were not. By using this information with an opportunity to practice skills, we worked to help participants gain a more balanced and optimistic outlook. According to their feedback, this seemed to be beneficial in the lives of many of these young people.

One of the observations of the global economic downturn of recent years was how unprepared we were for it and how to some extent the bubble was fuelled by rampant optimism with not enough appreciation that things could go wrong and investments can fall as well as rise. Essentially, optimism and pessimism can serve to protect us and give us a more balanced, realistic viewpoint. However, one downside is that because of the fallout of the economic downturn, people seem to have become more fearful about the future, and anxiety, fear and worry about the future appears to be more prevalent. However, as Daniel Gilbert's research in an earlier chapter outlines, we have simply no idea how we will cope if the worst should happen and may be surprised about the resilience and strength we can find in such situations.

From working with a number of people impacted by the economic downturn and recession either through loss of job or loss of business, better coping seems to be associated with building a close circle of helpful people around you, being honest about exactly how bad things have become with those who need to know, and not to expect to adjust to or come to terms too quickly with the situation. The thing not to do is to suffer in silence.

I have learned much from working with such people, especially around keeping things more simple (for example, solve one problem at at a time instead of being overwhelmed by many) and how success can come from a range of influences, such as one person who continued to try to offer good service to his customers and in this way re-grew a new business and generated a decent income again. By trying to simply make money, he may have missed this opportunity to learn that all he could really control was how much he focused on service rather than whether people would bring him business or not. This is a really interesting idea, and one which is well explored by John Kay in his book *Obliquity* (listed below).

Key Thought

> *"If you always do what you have always done, you will always get what you have always got."*

Anonymous

Looking for Inspiration?

Martin O'Neill, both in his playing career and as a manager, has shown a real aptitude for getting the best out of those around him. By focusing on performance, he has been very successful, whether leading smaller clubs such as Wycombe to the big time, taking Celtic to an unforgettable UEFA Cup Final or dealing with a succession of Premiership teams and squads, culminating in his recent appointment as manager of the Ireland team. As a player and manager noted for his thoughtfulness, his other key qualities include a keenness to learn from what has worked or not worked for him.

Things to try...

*Think about a setback in your life (we all have them!). What did you learn and what do you now do differently as a result of this? Did this setback eventually stand to you in performing better or making sounder decisions in the future? Did this setback allow you to eventually develop some new skills and become more effective?

*The biggest danger with setbacks is not only the distress and difficulties they can cause, but by us not learning anything from them. Are there things that have gone wrong for you and changes that you have not yet made as a result of this?

*The Positive Psychology book listed below is well worth a read in terms of helping to see your life more positively and generally contains lots of helpful tips, strategies and advice.

If you liked this you can also look up…

Kay, J. (2010) *Obliquity: Why are goals are best achieved indirectly.* London: Profile Books.

Leimon, A. & McMahon, G. (2009) *Positive psychology for dummies.* Chichester, West Sussex: Wiley.

Moss, S. (2010) *Martin O'Neill: The biography.* London: John Blake Publishing.

www.mindyourself.ie/www.apt.ac

Chapter 15
WHERE'S MY OXYGEN MASK?

A useful indication that someone is enjoying reasonably good mental health is their ability to make timely and (usually) accurate decisions about their life, including the hundreds of small decisions each of us must make to successfully negotiate our way through each day. If you spend time in the company of a person who is experiencing psychological distress, even the seemingly most mundane decision (for example, should I watch TV? should I have a cup of tea?) can be an excruciating experience. Similarly, if you watch a football game involving a team who are low in confidence and/or in fear that they are going to be heavily beaten, you can notice the heads go down, eye contact being avoided and players who are wary of taking possession in case they lose possession or have no one to pass to next.

Nothing in life or football stays the same, but players and teams who do better tend to more explicitly focus on and take responsibility for what they *can* control and influence, such as their fitness, game plan, set piece strategy and plan if they lose a player, go two goals behind or two goals in front. In life, taking responsibility for ourselves and our families, and if your job involves it taking responsibility for people you manage or supervise, is an important factor for several reasons - not least that many people find themselves in trouble with a major problem due partly to the fact that they did not deal with this when it posed a more minor problem (for example, not attending to an injury or sickness before the condition worsened, or avoiding financial difficulties while debt continues to build up).

Other examples of taking responsibility could include managing our money more closely if we have less money than we used to or keeping fit even if we no longer play in a team. However, for those of us who are parents, responsibility can be taken to an entirely new level. I recall my own sense of being overwhelmed on becoming a parent and wondering how I was going to be able to be responsible for this little person, and how scary that felt. As ever, advice from friends and family helped, most notably from one friend who sagely explained that from now on I would permanently feel a little tired! While many children and young adults remain at home with their parent(s) well past 18 years of age for a variety of reasons, Jon Kabat-Zinn says it well when he describes the parenting journey as an 18 year long Buddhist retreat where, as a parent, you will probably experience almost every imaginable emotion.

Parenting children, including those with particular or more intense needs, requires much energy, patience, forgiveness and hard work. You need to remind yourself that this is often a hard task, perhaps the most onerous task and greatest responsibility any of us can take on. Balancing the duties of being a parent means you will need to get adequate rest and to spend time with other people where children or parenting are not always discussed. Perhaps not surprisingly, a common finding of both research undertaken with parents and in speaking with parents as a psychologist is that they often report raising children (especially during adolescence) as the most stressful thing in their lives and yet rate raising those children as their greatest achievement.

Key Thought

"Put on your own oxygen mask before attending to your child!"

Airline Safety Announcement

Looking for Inspiration?

Zinedine Zidane was not only one of the finest players in a powerful French team that won a World Cup in 1998 and European Championship in 2000 but he also forged a reputation as an elegant player with superb vision, winning FIFA World Player of the Year on three occasions. He also gave master classes in taking responsibility by not just delivering consistently after Real Madrid bought him for 75,000,000 Euro in 2001, but by scoring twice in the 1998 World Cup Final against Brazil, even overcoming getting sick on the pitch to score a penalty to follow up a brilliant free kick in the 2004 European Championships. Despite a sad end to his international career at the 2006 World Cup, even then, Zidane had come out of international retirement to captain France to another World Cup Final, underling his own commitment and desire to take responsibility.

Things to try...

*Is there something important you have been putting off that you could do today?

*Your best resource as a parent is often other parents who may likely share the same worries, concerns and fears that you do. Spending time with these people to talk about our children and especially to talk about each other's interests is important.

*Sleep is crucial, especially if you have younger children, and take the chance to rest whenever you can and accept offers from trusted people to babysit when it suits you.

*Have a look at some of the useful parenting books below or try a useful parenting website such as supernanny.co.uk, familylives.org.uk, or stevebiddulph.com.

If you liked this you can also look up...
Biddulph, S. & Biddulph, S. (2003) *The complete secrets of happy children.* London: Thorsons.

Faber, A. & Mazlish, E. (2001) *How to talk so kids will listen and listen so kids will talk* London: Piccadilly Press.

Parker, J., Stimpson, J. & Rowe, J. (2010) *Raising happy children: What every child needs their parents to know – from 0-11 years* London: Hodder.

Kabat-Zinn, M. & Kabat-Zinn, J. (1997) *Everyday blessings: The inner work of mindful parenting.* New York: Hyperion.

Chapter 16

WATCH THE OFFSIDE TRAP

How often have you seen a really good opportunity spurned because the striker, whilst trying to get into the best position possible, has strayed a little too forward too soon and the cross comes in while the flag goes up for offside? Not only is this a deeply frustrating experience for all concerned, it is also such a waste of energy. As in life itself, the key in beating the offside trap is to be aware of where you are in relation to other people as you make your run. Run too early and the offside flag goes up, wait too long and you miss the cross.

In our own lives, we can become "offside" in our relationships by not being aware of where we are, or where we need to be in relation to others. I have a tendency to stay at work too long and when my family point this out, I feel as if I have strayed into an "offside position" as I was too focused on getting a particular piece of work completed without due regard for what my family needed (or what I had promised them, usually being home by a certain time).

Being home late is relatively easy to acknowledge, given the difference between the time I promised I would be home and the actual time I arrived home. What is much harder to figure out are the issues that can build up between us and others, that are more difficult to notice and as a result, more problematic to raise and discuss. For example, a colleague told me recently that another colleague had given them a "smirk" as they believed that the other person was aware of a setback this individual had experienced in work. When I spoke with the other person, they confirmed that they were aware of the bad news their colleague had received and so "smiled warmly" at this person, as a signal of support and solidarity. So one person's smirk can be another person's warm smile, but the danger is that if these issues are not addressed, then every subsequent interaction adds more fuel to the fire. Being "offside" with people, especially people we are usually close to or spend a lot of time with or depend on, tends to cause most of us a lot of distress.

Inside and outside of my work, including with families, I have seen this type of misunderstanding foster poor relations among and between groups of people over a prolonged period of time. This can often reach a point where it is very clear that there exists bad feeling between the people/group, but less certainty as to what the actual cause of this bad feeling was.

If we go out of our way to upset or annoy people, then we can generally expect turbulent and volatile interpersonal relationships with these people and those close to them. But all too often, perceived slights such as the one outlined above, are not reflected upon and remain unspoken. These can have devastating consequences for relationships. Equally, I have known situations where people are aware that they have hurt or upset others (or have being hurt or upset themselves), yet do nothing about the situation and let it fester as they do not want to face dealing with the situation or are not sure what to do about it. It is crucial to try to deal with such issues, and if your approaches to try to resolve the issue are not welcome or reciprocated, then at least you will have the consolation of knowing you have tried.

Key Thought

"To know when to go away and when to come closer is the key to any lasting relationship."

Domenico Cieri Estrada

Looking for Inspiration?

Karren Brady, is sometimes referred to as the "first lady of football", having been involved in the game for over 20 years. She has steered her clubs through a number of potentially difficult situations including, Birmingham City becoming a public listed company in 1997 (the club was in receivership when she became director in 1993), leading to her being the youngest Managing Director of a PLC. More recently, in her role as Vice-Chairman of West Ham United, she is involved in their proposed move to the London Olympic Stadium in 2016, again dealing with a range of complex and potentially difficult situations.

Things to try...

*If you get a feeling that someone is annoyed with you, or if you are told this by someone else, try to approach the person and ask to talk about this issue.

*Stick to the facts, not just your feeling or perception of what happened, and remember it is still possible to really like someone and yet be very angry at them over their behaviour.

What tends to cause most damage are extreme reactions (e.g. "I hate you" or "I will never talk to you again"). Be open to what the other person has experienced (this does not mean you are wrong) and meet again to see how you are doing with each other.

*Use "I" statements that reflect only what you think or feel and do not bring the opinions of people not present into the discussion as doing this rarely helps.

*The Skynner and Cleese book, listed below, is very helpful from a family perspective.

*When dealing with people who are simply rude, Lynne Truss's book (listed below) provides some useful ideas. Similarly, Robert Sutton has some helpful ideas for dealing with issues in the workplace.

If you liked this you can also look up...

Skynner, R. & Cleese, J. (1983) *Families and how to survive them.* London: Mandarin.

Sutton, R. (2007) *The no-asshole rule: Building a civilised workplace and surviving one that isn't.* London: Sphere.

Truss, L. (2006) *Talk to the hand: The utter bloody rudeness of everyday life.* London: Profile Books.

Chapter 17

YOU CAN'T WIN THEM ALL

Life tends to teach us that there are situations we encounter where we will not achieve what we wanted and there may not be much we can do about this. Even the very greatest football teams cannot keep winning, and where there is any sense of balance between the teams in a match, neither team will be on top for the full 90 minutes. This does not mean that we should not aim high or try to reach our goals, but be aware that we simply cannot win every time.

I used to see failure at any level (or indeed at anything) as some kind of personal wound that I had to hide away and be ashamed about. Yet as I get older, not meeting my goals every time and experiencing failure has brought some interesting (if painful!) learning. Firstly, there is a tendency not to change a winning team and therefore it is easier to spot weaknesses or problems in a team that is currently not successful. Secondly, if we are never 100% sure that we will win or lose each game (just notice how much more competitive the Premiership has become in recent years, with teams much more evenly balanced and results much harder to predict), then there is less to lose in any case. Importantly, I have also learned in life that there are some situations, where *no-one would have succeeded*, no matter how much effort or skill was applied.

In working with teams I like to use a forgiveness ritual before a game where the team look at each other and forgive each other in advance for the mistakes or errors they may make in the game ahead (including mistakes management may make in terms of tactics, formation or substitutions). This can help to settle players while highlighting the idea that mistakes or errors, especially in a very competitive and high stakes contest, are inevitable.

Failure can provide an opportunity to assess where we are and what we need to do. To ensure that it does not become a crushing experience, it is important not to expect too much every time, thus forcing further pressure upon ourselves. It is also crucial that we also give ourselves effort for *trying* as it is much easier to be part of a team that is winning, and practice compassion towards ourselves, instead of constant judgements for not being good enough. If you find this difficult, then it may be helpful to seek psychological therapy to address these issues, which may be part of a recurrent but upsetting pattern, possibly originating from earlier in your life.

Key Thought

"Nothing fails like success."

Anonymous

Looking for Inspiration?

Eamon Dunphy played in England for 17 seasons, moving to Manchester United as a schoolboy and finishing out his career in the lower divisions, finally returning to win an FAI Cup Medal with Shamrock Rovers in Dublin, the only such medal he won in his entire professional career. However, he continued to play despite the lack of medals. His story to date, told in his book *The Rocky Road,* is a very gritty, "warts and all" account of the ups and downs of being a professional player, and the highs and lows of spending a lifetime involved in football.

Things to try...

*Practice forgiveness regularly for yourself and be patient with yourself, we will all make mistakes and no one is perfect. If you are in a team try the forgiveness ritual, as outlined above, before a game.

*Openly talking about fear is much more helpful than trying to pretend it does not exist and if we check out the things we are worried about, we can usually plan better to deal with difficulties which may arise.

*Check out Paul Gilbert's book on cultivating compassion (listed below) and the story of Joe Kernan, an inspirational figure in Gaelic Football, who continues to contribute to sport despite setbacks in recent years.

If you liked this you can also look up...

Gilbert, P. (2009). *The compassionate mind*. London: Constable.

Kernan, J. & Breheny, M. (2011). *Without a shadow of a doubt*. Dublin: Irish Sports Publishing.

Klemmer, B. (2008). *The compassionate samurai*. London: Hay House.

Dunphy, E. (2013). *The rocky road*. Dublin: Penguin.

Chapter 18

OVER THE HILL?

One of the most common misperceptions is that football is a game purely for the younger person, and that once you have passed the first flush of youth that you can no longer contribute to, or enjoy football (or sport in general).

Thankfully, this does not have to be the case as we are generally living longer. As our life expectancy increases, if we can avoid serious accidents or serious illness, football can continue to play an important role in our lives. Many people who have enjoyed playing sports go on to help out their teams and clubs in a variety of roles after they stop playing, or in some cases, do so without having played at all. This could include helping out with coaching, managing, administering, fund-raising or providing other practical help. It can also include parents introducing their children to the teams they have themselves played with, allowing parents and children to enjoy this healthy common interest, while giving the child the possibility of a lifelong interest in sport and an insight into their parents' interests. Such input is often the lifeblood for teams and clubs, is very important in the lives of those who contribute, and tends to benefit the broader community.

Alongside the benefits of providing regular exercise, a chance to socialise and to give and receive support from others, playing football (or any sport) can be an important part of your weekly routine, and be a consistent fixture, even when other things in your life can change, including retirement. I am lucky to be part of a group who play five-a-side indoor football from September through to the following May (the summer and the longer evenings provides an opportunity for outdoor pursuits). The original group began playing in the weekly time slot over 30 years ago. One of the members of the group recently retired from his job and now speaks about how the football has become more important to him at a time when there have been so many other changes in his life and as he now sees people less than when he was working in a very busy job over the past number of years. He stays in very good shape and is ultra competitive despite being in his 60's, and likes to remind me that while I am younger than him, I am also slower!

This suggests that we may have more to look forward to as we grow older and as throughout the lifespan, football can provide a focal point for interest and activities. Celebrated German psychologist Paul Baltes dedicated much of his career to studying development across the life-cycle, particularly highlighting how we can become wiser as we grow older, and continue to contribute to the lives of those around us.

One of the enduring memories of my childhood is of helping in and around the family pub, and learning how important all sports were to the customers who came in. The days leading up to big matches were exciting with much debate about which team would win, but even more activity happened the day or two after when the post-mortems into the result would begin, the newspapers accounts of the action would be pored over, and often read triumphantly aloud. Certain people came into the pub more often and stayed for longer after their team had won, while supporters of the losing team may not have been seen for a while until things had died down a little.

What struck me most about those debates was how inclusive they were, and while not everyone drank alcohol, the debates about football and other sports always involved people from every walk of life and from across the age span, including those with and without jobs. As a teenager, without necessarily knowing these people well, I learned in those moments about the power of football and sport in general in providing a common language and understanding, and everyone was welcome into the debate as long they had an opinion of their own. For me, this remains one of the wonderful and most important things about being a football fan and a follower of sports in general.

Key Thought

"People do not quit playing because they grow old; they grow old because they quit playing."

Oliver Wendell Holmes

Looking for Inspiration?

Billy Bonds played for West Ham for over 20 years, enjoying huge personal success and probably improving as a player over time, playing his last game for the club in 1988 at Southampton in the top division of English Football at the remarkable age of 41 years and 226 days. Billy was an inspirational, charismatic and brave midfielder/defender, also captaining the club for 10 years and leading them to victory in the FA Cup in 1975 and 1980.

Things to try...

*Consider the last 5 or 10 years of your life and what would you think you have learned most in that time?

*"Wise Mind" is an important idea - what we get when we combine what our "head" says *with* what our "heart" says, try this and see how it works for you. We can run into problems when we are *too* thoughtful (from the head) or *too* emotional (from the heart), so this combination can almost always work well for us.

*One occupation that suits people who have lots of experience of football with a strong element of wisdom is refereeing, have a look at David Ellery's book (below) noting the ups and downs of a career never far from the spotlight.

If you liked this you can also look up...

Baltes, P. & Ulrich, K. (1998). *The Berlin aging study: Aging from 70 to 100*. Cambridge: Cambridge University Press.

Ellary, D. (2004). *The man in the middle*. London: Time Warner Books.

Pearsall, P. (1997). *Write your own pleasure prescription: 60 ways to create balance and joy in your life*. Alameda, CA: Hunter House.

Chapter 19

ALL TOGETHER NOW

In psychological therapy, a helpful and popular approach to helping people deal with problems and be happier in life is a form of talk therapy called Cognitive Behaviour Therapy (CBT). One of the key ideas in this approach is that early in life (or sometimes early in a new phase of life) we have important experiences which strongly influence how we expect life to be in the future - known as 'Core Beliefs' - which tend to stay the same across life, despite evidence that they may not reflect the reality of our lives now and/or be unhelpful to us. Unfortunately, if a person has negative or unhelpful core beliefs, these can persist across life in the same way positive ones can. So if you were to try to do some CBT with me you could see my support of West Ham as a Core Belief formed early in life and persisting throughout the years. You might also highlight the evidence that supports this belief (the FA Cup win in 1980) and the evidence that does not (not many trophies since then!), to help me arrive at a more balanced and helpful conclusion.

In trying to explain the idea of Core Beliefs, I have found it useful to compare it to the story of why someone supports a particular football team, which tends to be an event that happened early on in life and has some emotional connection, for example supporting a team because a relative or friend also supported the team. However, while evidence may persist that I may experience more success or happiness by supporting another team (in my case perhaps another London team such as Arsenal or Chelsea); I tend to stick with my support for West Ham whatever happens, but have to be prepared to live with the consequences of this.

Being part of something bigger than and outside of ourselves is a key human need for most people. This need may be met by being part of a family, community, church or religious group or organisation, and tends to be a more positive experience when we feel at home with like-minded people who accept us and our views, which then makes self-acceptance so much easier. Other positive experiences of this shared identity include a (sometimes) unspoken sense of comradeship and understanding when you meet another fan of your team, and a positive feeling when the team have a good result. The obvious downside is of course, the teasing and bragging of other team's fans when your team get beaten.

Being a football supporter and following a certain team also tends to involve a particular view of the world, instilling certain values within us as to how the team should play and what philosophy or approach should be employed. Essentially, these are important values that persist, and even as football is increasingly viewed as a global franchise with a sharp business element, the class and respect that emanates from players and supporters of all teams remembering each other's significant losses (for example, the 1958 Munich Air Crash or the 1996 Hillsborough Tragedy), or sending out a message of support to an unwell player (such as the Aston Villa fans "19" minute tribute for Stiliyan Petrov and his battle with leukaemia), reminds us that we are together in a broader football family, with more in common that we thought.

Key Thought

"Above all, I would like to be remembered as a man who was selfless, who strove and worried so that others could share the glory, and who built up a family of people who could hold their heads up high and say 'We're Liverpool'."

Bill Shankly

Looking for Inspiration?

Fabrice Muamba's extraordinary story of his heart stopping during a match between Wigan and Spurs and making a recovery, was both alarming and extraordinary. It was alarming in the sense that it was hard to believe that such a dynamic professional athlete could find himself in such a situation, and extraordinary in that it prompted a powerful response and appreciation among all football fans of the miracle witnessed that night and how ultimately, a life was saved on a football pitch.

Things to try...

*Try to think of what bonds football fans and players together?

*Ask yourself what does football add to your life? How different would your life be without it? What would you miss most about it?

*Reflect on the best things that being a football fan has brought you in life? Are there any downsides?

If you liked this you can also look up...

Kelly, S. (1997). *It's much more important than that: Bill Shankly, the biography.* London: Virgin Books.

Muamba, F. & Brereton, C. (2012). *I'm still standing: My incredible story.* Liverpool: Sport Media.

Wilson, R. & Branch, R. (2006). *Cognitive Behaviour Therapy for Dummies.* Chichester: Wiley.

Chapter 20

FORM IS TEMPORARY

In any sport, or indeed any game, a player or team can simply not always dominate the opposition and win every time. Players, like the rest of us, seem to have periods of their career where their motivation, fitness, team interplay, tactics and performance all come together to provide an almost unbeatable display. Exceptional players (and teams) seem much better able to keep all of these factors in harmony with each other more consistently than opponents, and this is often due to the efforts of the team management and coaches, helping them dominate games and seasons. However, this does not last forever as keeping all of the above elements is so difficult, and sometimes when a team has dominated for a period of time (for example, Liverpool after the 1980's) they can go for a lengthy period of time with little or none of the scale of the success they once enjoyed.

The difficulty is that, if you have enjoyed a period of success, then the expectations become heightened and all future events are measured against the past successes. We have seen this effect mirrored to a certain extent in the economy of many European countries since 2007/2008 when the economic bust followed the boom, and people were left not only in trying financial situations, but were making contrasts with what they may have had and then lost, adding to an overall sense of uncertainty and anxiety, and for some people, hopelessness.

There is truly something special then about a great player, team or manager reminding us that they still have the magic touch and what it takes, even if that is only in a glimpse and like all success, past or present, does not last forever. Succumbing to defeat and finishing out a career away from the bright lights and dizzy heights of success is human and few players go through a glittering career and still finish at the top.

Maybe it is how we like our heroes, in that we often become more attached to players, managers or teams who have the same kind of background or geographical base as us, making it easier to relate to them. If they do well and have wonderful careers then we appreciate this, but we look forward to them eventually returning to the places and people from where they came. In life, as in football, we are not always going to be successful or have our dreams fulfilled. Sometimes, when things are going our way and we are getting the things we need and having success, it could be seen as a good sequence of results or good run of form. But what if our run is halted and other factors intervene and despite trying our best, we just cannot seem to find our previous form. All we can do in such a situation is to keep trying and live up to what we value and hold to be important.

Brian Clough, in his lifetime, had setbacks and disappointments like we all do. But perhaps the difference between Brian and the rest of us is the amazing success he had in football, especially in the earlier part of his managerial career. While his success was carved out using a unique, inimitable approach (alongside Peter Taylor at Nottingham Forest), he continued to apply this approach for the rest of his managerial career, while some of the bigger clubs developed and spent money, eventually overcoming Forest, who only won a single championship in Clough's 16 years as manager. While his spell at Forest did ultimately end in failure with relegation from the First Division in 1993, he always did it his own way and never deviated from what he believed in. The lesson could be that form is temporary, but class is permanent - something in the ups and downs of life we could all learn from.

Key Thought

"I want no epitaphs of profound history and all that type of thing. I contributed - I would hope they would say that, and I would hope somebody liked me."

Brian Clough

Looking for Inspiration?

As Brian Clough said, all any of us can hope to do in life is make a contribution to a team, a relationship, a family, an organisation, a club. While he may not have enjoyed the dizzy heights of winning the First Division Championship a year after getting promoted from the Second Division and back to back European Cup successes later in his career, for me, Brian Clough remains the most intriguing and complex person in football history, as well known for what he said and how he managed, as for his incredible successes.

Even today his achievements at Nottingham Forest in particular are difficult to comprehend, where he took a team who had previously enjoyed a very modest degree of success, to winning the European Cup back to back (then played throughout in a more knockout style format), alongside one Championship and four League Cups. To look at it another way, how difficult would it be nowadays to win the Champions League back to back? How would we rate such a manager now?

Things to try...

*Be aware of and note the times in your life that you are enjoying success and be aware that this is down to a range of factors - when we are successful everything is not perfect for us, and when we lose not everything is wrong either.

*In times where you meet disappointment and even failure, remember the one factor we have most influence over and often the only one we can control, is our effort - one constant feature of successful teams is their ability to play for 90 minutes plus.

*If you want to find out more about what makes us tick, have a look at the fascinating book by Daniel Kahneman, a Nobel Prize winning psychologist.

If you liked this you can also look up...

Hamilton, D. (2007) *Provided you don't kiss me: 20 years with Brian Clough.* London: Fourth Estate.

Kahneman, D. (2011) *Thinking, fast and slow.* London: Allen Lane.

Lelord, F. (2010) *Hector and the search for happiness.* London: Gallic Books.

Chapter 21

IF THE GRASS IS ALWAYS GREENER

In his wonderful book on the life of George Best, *"Immortal"*, which was written with the approval and co-operation of George's family, Duncan Hamilton tells a powerful story. Duncan was visiting George's grave with members of George's family when four men in black suits approached the grave and said that they wanted to "say hello to George" and pay their respects to him, having been at a burial in another part of Roselawn cemetery in Belfast. As with any hero, people seem to feel a connection with George Best, whose difficulties were as well publicised as his brilliance, and fans feel they know him and worship him, yet most never had the chance to actually meet with or even see him in person.

George Best's story seems both triumphant and tragic, and he has remained an icon not only since his death, but through the slow decline in his fortunes from the glorious summit of 1968, when he inspired Manchester United to the European Cup, and in the same year picked up both the Ballon d'Or and FWA Footballer of the year. Incredibly and sadly, he never won another major honour in the game (although he was 3rd in the Ballon d'Or in 1971). Every football fan will have their favourite George Best story, game, moment or goal.

The abiding memories, for me, are his performance in a superb 2-2 draw between Northern Ireland and Holland in 1976 (including a nutmeg on Johan Cruyff) and an incredible individual goal he scored for the San Jose Earthquakes against Fort Lauderdale Strikers in the North American Soccer League in 1981. For me, a sign of the man's enduring talent and class was that both these games took place much later in George's career, when most pundits would generally agree he was not at the peak of his powers.

Listen to most conversations among football fans about George's life and career, and you will likely hear people talk about how his potential remained unfulfilled and how was never able to re-capture the wonderful success of 1968. In some ways the saddest thing about George's story is that given his glittering success in the earlier part of his career (certainly up to 1968), that it was always going to be difficult to live up to those standards and reach those heights again. Similarly, George had prospered and developed under Matt Busby; the man who signed him gave him his debut and had him as an integral part of his European Cup winning team. George seemed to lose his way somewhat when his mentor stepped aside, the man who knew and understood him so well, and this seemed to be an important factor in George struggling in the years afterwards, up until he left Manchester United.

The themes in this story can sometimes be seen in the lives of people who are dissatisfied, disgruntled or distressed in their lives. One of the super highways to unhappiness is to constantly compare yourself with anyone, including with yourself, for example when you were younger or fitter. I have seen so many people make their own lives more difficult by constantly making comparisons with others (or with themselves at a different stage), not focusing or not focusing enough on what is positive, healthy, satisfying, important or hopeful in their own life.

Often the problem is that the person simply does not even fully notice or acknowledge the strengths or positives in their life; instead only noticing what they think may be missing or may be wrong. Central to this, is the perception (often an inaccurate one), that other peoples' lives are better than ours because they appear to be so. One of the enduring lessons from my work as a psychologist, with the privilege of getting to know people often at a vulnerable time and hearing very sensitive things about them, is that people's lives are not always as fulfilled or complete as they may appear from a distance.

Equally problematic is some people's sense of entitlement, believing that it is their right to have certain things in life (such as having a good job or a nice place to live). Sport teaches us that no person or team are entitled to anything and that life is not always fair. Usually hard work is required to attain success, and perhaps harder work to hold onto it. In such instances it is important to look at our own situation and make the most of what we have been given and what we have; there will always be someone who appears better off than we are.

Key Thought

> *"If the grass if always greener on the other side, maybe you are not looking after your own patch well enough."*

William Davies

Looking for Inspiration?

Matt Busby could well have felt that he would do better at another club when offered the Real Madrid job in 1956. However, major trauma was visited upon Manchester United returning from a game against Red Star Belgrade in the 1958 Munich air crash, when his "Busby Babes" lost seven players and three club officials. Not aware of the full extent of the tragedy for a number of weeks afterwards, Matt Busby nearly died himself and some reports suggest that he may have blamed himself to some degree for what happened (he had been very keen for Manchester United to compete in the European Cup). Despite this, he set about the rebuilding of the club and his team, and with the FA Cup and First Division Championship providing stepping stones, this process culminated with winning the European Cup in 1968.

Things to try...

*Have a look at the George Best This is Your Life rare footage on YouTube. Also look up the Northern Ireland and Holland game from 1976 and the wonderful individual goal he scored for the San Jose Earthquakes against Fort Lauderdale Strikers from 1981.

*Have a look at the "Enjoy every sandwich" book listed below which is a powerful story about making the most of life when we have it.

*If you were to "look after your own patch better" what could you start with? Is there an area of life that you have been neglecting and that you could invest some time in, for example getting regular exercise, time with an important person or developing a skill or idea that you have?

If you liked this you can also look up...
Dunphy, E. (2007) *A strange kind of glory: Manchester United and Sir Matt Busby* (updated edition) London: Aurum Press.

Hamilton, D. (2013) *Immortal: The approved biography of George Best.* London: Century.

Lipsenthal, L. (2012) *Enjoy every sandwich: Living each day as if it were your last.* London: Bantam Press.

Parkin, John (2007) *F**K It: The ultimate spiritual way.* London: Hay House.

Chapter 22

PUTTING IT ALL TOGETHER:
TRUST

In this final chapter of the book, I have tried to take some of the overall themes in the previous chapters and put them together in a way you can hopefully relate to and take with you, perhaps like the last words before leaving the dressing room before a game. In my experience, many people seem to find it helpful to be able to take such a message or learning away in the form of a mantra or mnemonic, and for me this is instilled in the following:

Tactics

Although "going with the flow" and being "easy going" has many advantages, when facing challenges in life, and when attempting to overcome difficulties or trying to win a football match, a game plan is required, including "what if" sections (for example in football, what do we do if we go 2-0 down? Have a player sent off? Lose our goal keeper to injury?), where we need to adjust our plans as circumstances change. Game plans also outline what we need to do, why we need to do it, when we need to do it, where we need to do it and with whom. Within a team, plans have to be clear, agreed and absorbed. This takes time, and is always worth doing. Any of the great upsets in the modern game, where the ability of one team was thought far superior to the other, were based on a clear game plan, along with the confidence that the plan was workable.

Tactics and clear plans help us be clear about what, why and how we approach situations, and help sharpen and maintain our focus. Tactics change as a situation develops, and new experiences now can lead to new or different tactics in the future.

Rehearsal

Preparation and practice are key ingredients in any match situation, as they are in life itself. We are more effective in football by continuously rehearsing situations we know we will experience (for example, corner kicks or free kicks) or skills we require (for example, shooting or heading). In life we can become more effective by getting into good habits that help us get what we want or need, or that help us feel better about ourselves (for example, regular exercise or getting important work done), while trying to avoid bad habits (for example drinking to excess or postponing tasks we do not like) that can distract us from our goals. Being better able to concentrate on what goes on around us and being mindful and clear within our own heads, can help us to deal better when something unexpected occurs. Rehearsal also helps us address concerns about our ability or resources more directly, meaning we deal with the fears we can deal with, and not letting these completely take over.

The more we rehearse for a situation or task, and support this by building good habits that help us achieve this, and avoiding those habits that do not help, while balancing our fears and worries, the more effective we will be.

Understanding

Every person and every team is different, and very few if any situations we face in life are exactly the same. Getting to know ourselves and those around us helps us get into a better position to figure out what makes us tick as people, how our past can influence our present and why we feel certain ways about things. Importantly, this can also allow us have a better understanding of other people and be more aware of this in our relationships, leaving room for what it is we do not know (and may never know) about others. It also helps to understand what we have to do and when.

Context is crucial in football and life and us having a good sense of ourselves, other people, our team, organisation or family can help us be more able to perform, and being clear about what we have to do makes us more effective.

Strengths

We will never win a game if we only focus on stopping the other team from playing and trying not to let our weaknesses be exposed. Not only do we need to be aware of what our strengths are, but we need to nurture these and practice using them, both individually and with the team. Importantly playing to our strengths also gives us more confidence, helps us be less anxious and can help us have more influence. Sometimes when we are part of a team, family or organisation, getting the best out of a situation means prioritising one set of strengths over another depending on the circumstances, and just because we are good at one task or in one area, this does not mean that we always have to display that strength every time.

Recognising, nurturing and finally playing to our strengths means that we have a better chance of succeeding. A strong team are able to prioritise which strengths are best suited to each challenge, and when to use and not to use these.

Together

Loneliness and isolation can do huge damage in our lives, and life is usually much better when we are around people we care about and get on with. Ask ex-footballers what they miss most after retiring, and the common answer is the camaraderie of the dressing room, often ranking above their victories and achievements. As a team game, we cannot succeed in football as an individual, much as in life itself, and we are at our strongest as part of a network of others, and while we may have our dysfunctions and upsets with other people, it helps to keep trying to repair any difficulties between us as they arise.

Being with people we feel a sense of connection with and share a purpose with is very good for your health. It is also the key focus of any team sport, and central to every winning team.

Putting it all together:

> **T**actics
> **R**ehearsal
> **U**nderstanding
> **S**trengths
> **T**ogether

The key element is to remember to trust yourself, your team-mates and those around you, for without trust we would not have teamwork, togetherness or any shared sense of purpose. While there is a danger our trust will be misplaced, without trust we can do little in football and little in life.

Good Luck!

Acknowledgements

Grateful thanks and appreciation..

To my parents Eddie & Kathleen for their love and the sacrifices they made.

To my family, friends and colleagues for all your patience, kindness and helpful suggestions when I bored you with ideas about this book over the past number of years.

To all the people who contributed to my training in Queens University and Trinity College, especially my lecturers, tutors, supervisors and classmates. I learned about psychology and so much more from you. Particular thanks to the Assistant and Trainee Psychologists I have had the privilege of working with.

To everyone associated with Mind Yourself and Back of the Net, for showing me what was possible. To Julia and John who encouraged me to write a paper on adolescent psychotherapy which led directly to this book.

To Amy and all at APT, especially Will, my mentor.

To my colleagues and friends who read the manuscript, and offered helpful feedback and support.

To Garrett and Steven at Original Writing, for all their assistance and advice.

To all the fabulous players, coaches, managers, clinicians, researchers and authors who have helped shape this book, if I have found a different vantage point it is because I am standing on the shoulders of giants.

To all the people I have had the honour of working with as a psychologist...thank you for the opportunity to walk part of the way with you, for the invaluable lessons you have taught me and for your contribution to this book.

Abrahams, D. (2012) *Soccer tough: Simple football psychology techniques to improve your game.* Birmingham: Bennion Kearny.

Babuta, L. (2009) *The power of less: The 6 essential productivity principles that will change your life.* London: Hay House.

Balague, G. (2012) *Pep Guardiola: Another way of winning: the biography.* London: Orion Books.

Balauge, G. (2013) *Messi* London: Orion Books.

Baltes, P. & Ulrich, K. (1998) *The Berlin ageing study: Aging from 70 to 100.* Cambridge: Cambridge University Press.

Beck, A.T. (1988) *Love is never enough: How couples can overcome misunderstandings, resolve conflicts, and solve relationships through cognitive therapy.* New York: HarperPerennial.

Biddulph, S. & Biddulph, S. (2003) *The complete secrets of happy children.* London: Thorsons.

Bjergegaard, M. & Milne, J. (2013) *Winning without losing.* London: Profile Books.

Bregman, P. (2011) *18 minutes: Find your focus, master distractions & get the right things done.* London: Orion Books.

Brooks, D. (2011) *The social animal: A story of how success happens.* New York: Random House.

Burch, V. & Penman, D. (2013) *Mindfulness for health: a practical guide to relieving pain, reducing stress and restoring wellbeing.* London: Piatkus.

Cade, B. and O'Hanlon, W. H. (1993) *A brief guide to brief therapy.* New York, W.W. Norton.

Cain, S. (2012) *Quiet: The power of introverts in a world that can't stop talking.* London: Penguin.

Davies, W. (2000) *Overcoming anger and irritability: A self-help guide using cognitive behavioural techniques.* London: Robinson.

Davies, W. (2013) *The RAID course handbook.* Leicester: APT Press.

Dobelli, R. (2013) *The art of thinking clearly.* London: Sceptre.

Dunphy, E. (2007) *A strange kind of glory: Manchester United and Sir Matt Busby* (updated edition) London: Aurum Press.

Dunphy, E. (2013) *The Rocky Road.* Dublin: Penguin.

Dweck, C. (2006) *Mindset: how you can fulfil your potential.* New York: Random House.

Ellary, D. (2004) *The man in the middle*. London: Time Warner Books.

Ferguson, A. (2013) *My autobiography*. London: Hodder & Stroughton.

Forsyth, J.P. & Eifert, G.H (2007) *The mindfulness & acceptance workbook for anxiety*. Oakland, CA: New Harbinger.

Gaffney, P. (2010). The Teenage Psychotherapy First XI: On learning from the beautiful game. *Counselling Psychology Review, 25,* 1, 6 – 12.

Gilbert, D. (2006) *Stumbling on Happiness*. New York: Random House.

Gilbert, P. (2009) *The compassionate mind*. London: Constable.

Gladwell, M. (2013) *David & goliath*. London: Allen Lane.

Gerrard, S. & Winter, H. (2006) *Gerrard: My autobiography*. Bantam Press; London.

Faber, A. & Mazlish, E. (2001) *How to talk so kids will listen and listen so kids will talk* London: Piccadilly Press.

Hamilton, D. (2007) *Provided you don't kiss me: 20 years with Brian Clough*. London: Fourth Estate.

Hamilton, D. (2013) *Immortal: The approved biography of George Best.* London: Century.

Hardy, L. (2009) *Stokoe, Sunderland and 73: The story of the greatest FA Cup final shock of all time.* Orion: London.

Harris, R. (2008) *The Happiness trap: How to stop struggling and start living.* Boston: Trumpeter.

Hayes, S. & Smith, S. (2005) *Get out of your mind and into your life: The new acceptance & commitment therapy.* Oakland, CA: New Harbinger.

Holloway, I. & Clayton, D. (2008) *The little book of Ollie'isms.* Swindon: Green Umbrella Publishing.

Holloway, I., Clayton, D. & Francis, G. (2009) *Ollie: The autobiography of Ian Holloway.* Chelmsford: G2 Entertainmnent.

Jones, D (2009) *No smoke, no fire: the autobiography of Dave Jones.* Birmingham: Know the Score Books.

Joseph, S. (2011) *What doesn't kill us: The new psychology of posttraumatic growth.* New York: Basic Books.

Kabat-Zinn, M. & Kabat-Zinn, J. (1997) *Everyday blessings: The inner work of mindful parenting.* New York: Hyperion.

Kabat-Zinn, J. (2013) *Full catastrophe living (updated & revised).* New York: Bantam Books.

Kahneman, D. (2011) *Thinking, fast and slow.* London: Allen Lane.

Kay, J. (2010) *Obliquity: Why are goals are best achieved indirectly.* London: Profile Books.

Kelly, S. (1997) *It's much more important than that: Bill Shankly, the biography.* London: Virgin Books.

Kernan, J. & Breheny, M (2011) *Without a shadow of a doubt.* Dublin: Irish Sports Publishing.

Kopp, S. (1972) *If you meet the Buddha on the road, kill him!: The pilgrimage of psychotherapy patients* Palo Alto: Science and Behaviour Books.

Kopp, S. (1991) *All god's children are lost but only a few can play the piano.* New York: Prentice Hall Press.

Klemmer, B. (2008) *The compassionate samurai.* London: Hay House.

Leimon, A. & McMahon, G. (2009) *Positive psychology for dummies.* Chichester, West Sussex: Wiley.

Lelord, F. (2010) *Hector and the search for happiness.* London: Gallic Books.

Lipsenthal, L. (2012) *Enjoy every sandwich: Living each day as if it were your last.* London: Bantam Press.

Lois, G. (2012) *Damn good advice (for people with talent).* London: Phaidon Press.

Lowe, S. (2012) The brain in Spain, in *The Blizzard, 1*, 55-65.

Muamba, F. & Brereton, C. (2012) *I'm still standing: My incredible story.* Liverpool: Sport Media.

Merson, P. & Allen, M. (2012) *How not to be a professional footballer.* London: Harper Sport.

McConville, O. & McKenna, E. (2007) *The Gambler: Oisín McConville's story.* Edinburgh: Mainstream Publishing.

McGale, N., McArdle, S. & Gaffney, P. (2011) Exploring the effectiveness of an integrated exercise/CBT intervention for young men's mental health. *British Journal of Health Psychology, 16,* 3, 457-471.

Moss, S. (2010) *Martin O'Neill: The biography.* London: John Blake Publishing.

Neil, M. (2007) *Feel happy now!* London: Hay House.

Nhat Hanh, T. (2008) *The miracle of mindfulness.* London: Rider.

Norcross, J. & Guy, J. (2007) *Leaving it at the office: A guide to psychotherapist self-care.* New York: Guildford Press.

Nugent, R. & Brown, S. (2008) *Football: Raise your mental game.* London: A. & C. Black.

Parker, J., Stimpson, J. & Rowe, J. (2010) *Raising H a p p y Children: What every child needs their parents to know – from 0-11 years* London: Hodder.

Parkin, John (2007) *F**K It: The ultimate spiritual way.* London: Hay House.

Pearsall, P. (1997) *Write your own pleasure prescription: 60 ways to create balance and joy in your life.* Alameda, CA: Hunter House.

Pearsall, P. (2003) *The Beethoven factor: The new positive psychology of hardiness, happiness, healing and hope.* Charlottesville, VA: Hampton Roads.

Pearsall, P. (2005) *The last self-help book you'll ever need.* New York: Basic Books.

Peters, S. (2012) *The chimp paradox.* London: Vermilion.

Pink, D.H. (2010) *Drive: The surprising truth about what motivates us.* Edinburgh: Canongate.

Postma, A. (2013) *The power of acceptance.* London: Watkins Publishing.

Prochaska, J., Norcross, J. and DiClemente, C. (1994). *Changing for Good.* New York, Avon.

Putnam, R. (2000) *Bowling alone: The collapse and revival of American community.* New York: Simon and Schuster Paperbacks.

Reng, D. (2011) *A life too short: the tragedy of Robert Enke.* London: Yellow Jersey Press.

Scally, J. (2009) *A load of balls: Football's funny side.* Edinburgh: Mainstream Publishing.

Seligman, M (2002) *Authentic happiness: Using the new positive psychology to realise your potential for lasting fulfilment.* New York: Simon & Schuster.

Shapiro, F. (2012) *Getting past your past: Take control of your life with self-help techniques from EMDR therapy.* Emmaus, Pennsylvania: Rodale.

Sheard, M. (2010) *Mental toughness: The mindset behind sporting achievement.* Hove, Sussex: Routledge.

Shenk, D. (2010) *The genius in all of us.* London: Icon Books.

Skynner, R. & Cleese, J. (1983) *Families and how to survive them.* London: Mandarin.

Sutton, R. (2007) *The no-asshole rule: Building a civilised workplace and surviving one that isn't.* London: Sphere.

Sutton, R. (2012) *Good boss, bad boss: How to be the best...and learn from the worst.* New York: Business Plus.

Swales, M.A. & Heard, H.L. (2009) *Dialectical behaviour therapy: Distinctive features.* Hove, Sussex: Routledge.

Taleb, N.N. (2012) *Antifragile: Things that gain from disorder.* London: Penguin.

Templar, R. (2003) *The rules of work.* London: Pearson Education.

Tolle, E. (2006) *A new earth: Awakening to your life's purpose.* London: Plume.

Tracy, B. (2001) *Eat that frog.* San Francisco: Hodder Mobius.

Truss, L. (2006) *Talk to the hand: The utter bloody rudeness of everyday life.* London: Profile Books.

Van Gelder, K. (2010) *The Buddha and the Borderline.* Oakland, CA: New Harbinger.

Wilson, R. & Branch, R. (2006) *Cognitive Behaviour Therapy for Dummies.* Chichester: Wiley.

Dr. Paul Gaffney is a Clinical Psychologist who works primarily with vulnerable children and adolescents, and those who care for them. He was born in Keady, Co. Armagh and completed his Psychology degree at Queen's University Belfast, and Masters in Counselling Psychology and Doctorate in Clinical Psychology at Trinity College Dublin, where he remains an honorary tutor involved in the training of psychologists. He is a Registered Clinical Psychologist with the Psychological Society of Ireland and Chartered Psychologist with the British Psychological Society, and lives in Cavan.

He helped develop both "Mind Yourself", an evidence based positive mental health project which has been delivered to over 9,000 young people in Ireland, and "Back of the Net", an exercise/mental health project which has utilised a combination of football/exercise/cognitive behavioural therapy as a promising treatment for depression in young men. He is a Consultant Tutor with the Association for Psychological Therapies (APT), training mental health professionals internationally, and he enjoys a broad range of research and clinical interests, especially making effective mental health interventions more readily and broadly accessible.